Praise for Stephanie Pletka and Living Your Best Life

"LIVING YOUR BEST LIFE is a game-changer for women who struggle with finding their identity and living life to the fullest amid self-doubt, fear, guilt, and comparison. We've all been there. We can easily lose our sense of self and purpose in the maze of motherhood and marriage, and in the chaos of change. Written with southern humor, grit, and authenticity, this book is like having a conversation with a good friend who gets you. Stephanie's personal stories will capture your heart as she keeps her life real and relatable, tying it all together as she guides you with biblical principles, and practical application, to begin LIVING YOUR BEST LIFE! This book is a keeper!"

—Susan Miller, President of Just Moved Ministry & Author *After the Boxes are Unpacked*

"As moms, it's easy to find ourselves stuck, exhausted, and overwhelmed at every turn, as we lose our sense of identity. Stephanie reminds us that we are more than the roles we play and the hats we wear. With humor and truth, she helps us expose the lies we tell ourselves, empowering us to write our story and live an authentic, Christ-filled life with passion and purpose."

—Karen Stubbs, Founder of *Birds on a Wire*

"I love Stephanie's heart, encouraging women to live their best lives. I've watched her walk out the message of this book in her own life for years. Stephanie is the real deal. She gives voice to things we are all thinking and feeling and addresses the lies we believe with hard-hitting truth, wit, and laugh-out-loud humor. It is an honor to call her friend."

—Misty Phillip, The Struggle is Real but So Is God and host of the *By His Grace Podcast*

"With honesty, humor, and vulnerability, Stephanie weaves together personal stories and biblical truths into this book that will make you laugh, reflect, and will endear you to her. LIVING YOUR BEST LIFE exposes the lies that we so easily can fall prey to and reminds us to embrace life's imperfections while leaning on the Lord."

—Amy Carney, Author *Parent on Purpose:* A Courageous Approach to Raising Children in a Complicated World

LIVING YOUR BEST LIFE

Letting Go of Self-Doubt, Fear and
Other's Expectations to Live the Life
You've Always Dreamed

No one gets to tell you how your journey is written. Write your story. Stephanie :)

STEPHANIE PLETKA

PUBLISHED BY AUTHOR ACADEMY ELITE

AUTHOR ACADEMY elite

Published by Author Academy Elite.

Book Cover Design by Daliborka Mijailovic.

Author Photo credit: Ava Pletka

ISBN Hardback 978-1-64085-979-1 (Hardback)

ISBN Paperback 978-1-64085-978-4 (Paperback)

ISBN eBook 978-1-64085-980-7 (eBook)

Library of Congress Cataloging - in -Publication Data

Library of Congress Control Number: 2019916156

The events and stories in this book are from my perspective. Specific names may have been changed to protect the identities of those involved.

Printed in the United States of America

19 20 21 22 23 PC / WOR 10 9 8 7 6 5 4 3 2

Dedication

To John, my best friend, who I met on a bus in Tulsa all those years ago. You taught me what Partnership looks like and how to dream BIG.
I Love Us.

CONTENTS

TRANSITION 3: BECOMING

INTRODUCTION
WELCOME TO YOUR NEW START!

What if it's possible that who you are is who you are meant to be? You've picked up this book, looking for an answer, looking for a fresh start, for someone to tell you that you're doing a great job, that what you're doing matters, that you're not the only one going through tough times. I'll tell you stories in hopes of making you laugh, cry, and think. They won't be in any particular order, but stories used to prove a point. You may read this book and believe I have a camera focused on your life. You may shake your head, thinking, "Yes, this is me." Well, I've been there. I've been the mom who struggles to find some semblance of her old life, as I walk into the new one. I've been the mom who is questioning if what I am doing is right. If what I'm doing is enough. In this book, we'll deal with all the seasons and transitions associated with being a mom. As a Christian who's been down the gauntlet of life's tributaries, it's been my calling to write, represent, and be an advocate for all the moms, as you transition from one season of motherhood to another, always learning, growing, and becoming. I want to remind you that you are responsible for your happiness, that you are the one who gets to say how your story is written.

I write and speak, in hopes of bringing to light what we don't talk about. Those exposed, raw moments that isolate us from the pack. The hard things that make us compare ourselves to others, as a measuring stick of success. We all want to belong, to connect. However you became a mama, it's a members-only club, exclusive to those whose hearts have grown bigger, who would fight to their death, to save those kids that make you the happiest and craziest on the planet. I'm here to be your greatest cheerleader, your biggest fan, but also a big sister who's here to remind you not to believe the lies of self-doubt. The truth is, you are stronger than you think. You're a warrior, a fighter. You push strollers and shepherd hearts, feed, love, and nurture. As an entrepreneur, who had four kids in seven years, it was hard, y'all. No one can fully prepare you for the road ahead. The tough days of waking up at the crack of dawn or staying up until the wee hours, as you change diapers or wait for your teen to start a dialogue.

How did I come to write this book? I needed answers, so I began pouring through every article, website, and parenting book for solutions. And what worked for one child, didn't work for the other. So, I began to write, like the free therapy that it was. How many ways to cook a chicken, how to encourage teen communication, how to delegate chores for different ages and stages. When something worked for me, I posted it to my blog.

The craft sites taught me how to perfectly design the world's most fabulous birthday party in an old barn with the precise amount of dangling Edison lights. While the laundry room, with clothes stacked knee-deep, emphasized the chaos of my life. It's the little lies that hold us captive, hindering us from living our best life. Why am I writing this book before the sun rises, in my office, on a park bench, in every coffee shop, bookstore, scribbling on a notepad in the night? It's to remind you that you ARE enough that you HAVE what it takes. Instead of pounding ourselves for not being the world's greatest something, let us bestow kindness and grace. Let us give ourselves breathing room to enjoy the journey.

You can do the hard things. You can be so much more tomorrow than you were today. Don't give up, and don't give in. The best years are ahead. In the following chapters, I'll dispel the self-doubt we tell ourselves and offer steps that I've found helpful in turning my perspective around, in an unknown world where life is continually changing. As women, we are forever maneuvering into new territories and stages of life, navigating, and recalculating our position: Learning, Growing, and Becoming. It's time to make the change, to be the change, and write your story. Here's to Living Your Best Life.

Stephanie

TRANSITION 1

LEARNING

CHAPTER 1

FINDING YOUR TRIBE

You are the average of the five people
you most associate with.

~Tim Ferriss~

I burned down a barn. It wasn't actually my fault, per se. One moment, my nine-year-old self was jumping on a trampoline in the backyard of the trailer park where I grew up. The next, I was hearing the sirens of the fire truck that was putting out the flames of my neighbor's barn.

I grew up in the South, in the backwoods, off the banks of the Alabama River, chasing lightning bugs, fishing for catfish, and riding bikes till dusk. Life was my oyster, and I was as happy as a flea on a blue tick hound.

My favorite days included a good swimming hole, peach ice cream, and a song by Rick Springfield. The summer of 1980 had the makings of an epic adventure.

My best friend had stopped by to shoot the breeze and come up with a plan for the day. With curly blond hair and as feisty as she was skinny, she said:

"Hey, Stephanie. You won't believe what I did this morning."

"What trouble did you get into now?" I asked.

"You know those Winston cigarettes that Grandma smokes every day? The ones she would trade me in for, to get two more packs?"

"Yeah."

"I stole them from her kitchen windowsill this morning, and she's as mad as a wet hen. I want to smoke a cigarette and see what all the fuss is about."

After much negotiation on her part, we walked over to her grandma's barn and closed the double doors. My sole purpose in being there was for support. I had no intention of smoking a cigarette. My mission that day included jumping on a trampoline and building pine tree forts—and now there I was, sidetracking my potential. Like an episode of THE GOONIES, half of the neighborhood kids from ages eight to twelve were already in the barn hatching a plan. I couldn't believe my eyes, watching a kid smoke a cigarette. It was shocking. She asked me to try one. "No way," I said. "I'm a good girl. I'm nine."

But then she double-dog dared me. And y'all, if you're Southern, you don't take those challenges lightly. Do you think Reese Witherspoon's character in SWEET HOME ALABAMA, would have backed down from a double-dog dare? Or Reese herself, for that matter. No way. If word got out that you failed the challenge, your reputation was at stake. So, I caved and held the cigarette between my thumb and finger, like I was smoking weed. I had no idea how to hold a cigarette and only knew my way was wrong when a twelve-year-old began making fun of me. Instead of taking a small puff, I inhaled it like it was my last breath. I thought for sure I was dying, turning three shades of green with regret settling in. As the cigarette changed hands, something grabbed my attention. This barn was filled with canned vegetables, tomatoes, green beans, and corn. Hanging from the rafters were large pieces of salted meat. And stacked on the shelves were fifty or sixty mason jars filled with pee. Why would someone seal pee in a canning jar? We didn't have an answer. I mean, we were nine.

As I leaned down to discern the jars' contents, a neighborhood kid tossed a lit match, which landed in the open container. Boom! The explosion was deafening. The blast thrust me out the front door and into the wet grass. With singed eyebrows, and cheeks masked with soot, I coughed up black smoke. The barn was on fire, and our only recourse was to run. And run we did – in every direction like a stirred-up ant bed. It looked like a prison break. As I rounded the corner, my mom hollered my name. "What's the commotion?" she asked. "The barn is on fire." She knelt down, inspected my burned bangs, and asked, "Did you have anything to do with this?" I looked straight into her hazel eyes and emphatically said, "No ma'am." I'm not sure she believed me that day, but she wanted to enough that we never spoke of it again.

After the investigation, they discovered the mason jars contained moonshine, white lightning, 100 proof alcohol. I laid in bed that night and accessed my situation. Perhaps I needed new friends. How had I allowed myself to walk so far off the beaten path, that we burned down a barn? Instead of writing my own story, I gave someone else the power to determine its course. Something had to change. I needed a new tribe.

Now twenty-five years later, married with four kids, I wrestled again with finding the right tribe. I sat on the end of my bed, crying in despair. I had a good life and a supportive spouse, but something was missing. I had started a video production company years earlier. With the juggles and struggles of work-family balance and figuring out how many ways to cook a chicken, keeping up with appearances seemed an impossible task. I felt hopeless, overwhelmed, and isolated. Don't get me wrong, there were people all around, but the connection of a strong sisterhood was missing. Deep-rooted relationships had fallen by the wayside. I had become an expert plate spinner, swirling in organized chaos, but it turned out, it was just chaos.

Suddenly, I found myself separated from the human race. Little beings needed my full attention, and sleepless nights had become the lowly standard. Primary-colored toys filled my shabby chic living room. My life felt like herding cats in a rainstorm. No one came out unscathed. How did I get here? It felt like I was standing in that barn all those years ago, sidetracked from my potential. I was no longer in control of my life; instead, it was in control of me. My carpool attire had descended to torn boxer shorts and yesterday's makeup. Did anyone else feel like me?

Before kids, my husband and I had lived footloose and fancy-free. The sky was our limit. As newlyweds, John and I sat in the living room of our first home in Houston, Texas, on our green-and-white plaid couch, toasting to freedom with a box of wine and nachos for dinner. We raced in triathlons on the weekends and eventually adopted a dog. Whew, who knew how much sacrifice it took to care for a rambunctious dog? (As I write that, I laugh whole-heartedly at our cluelessness of what was to come.)

In the blink of an eye, we found ourselves with a mortgage, four kids, and two entrepreneurial start-ups. Suddenly, I was the ringmaster of a circus, sitting in isolation, unprepared for all the madness and mayhem. And that's when I heard the phrase; You are not enough. I spent days beating myself up, always thinking I should be further along in life. This phrase of self-doubt ran a loop in my head, like a bad sitcom rerun. What does "enough" look like? It's such an immeasurable term. Enough is defined as "adequate," and yet somehow, I viewed myself as inadequate, as if wearing anything less than a superhero cape meant I was letting the world down. What society once considered over-achievement had become the norm. I wondered, does anyone else feel this way, or am I the only one? I found myself in a vulnerable place, reaching out to other moms for advice, tips, and authenticity.

It took me back to the time when my first-born was six months old. My life felt like a blur, a brain fog of epic proportions. I met a woman from church who seemed to have a perfectly put-together life. She had no complaints, and everything seemed easy for her. Obviously, she was my answer. She brought warm, homemade blueberry muffins to bible study every week, with kids in tow and a smile on her face. Life looked effortless. I thought I'LL HAVE WHAT SHE'S HAVING, PLEASE. I invited her to lunch and shared my story. In my vulnerability and tears, overwhelmed and exhausted, I carefully placed my pain in her hands.

I shared my struggles of sleepless nights, midnight feedings, and the tough transition of being a stay-at-home mom. I recognized that my old life was gone, and I felt guilty for wanting it back. With anger in her voice, she said, "I have no idea what you're talking about." She looked perplexed, even annoyed as if the persona she had so meticulously created had cracked—otherwise, how could I think she had gone through similar circumstances? I left that day feeling like a lonely puppy that had been dropped off on the side of the road. I felt hopeless. I had placed my vulnerability in the hands of someone who didn't deserve it, unqualified to hold something so precious. I walked away from lunch, with tears flowing, placing my son in his little car seat. I felt more isolated than ever. I packed my feelings, my heart, my vulnerability into a closet of confinement, and silently suffered for more than a year, which catapulted me into further isolation.

As our little brood grew, matters only got worse. Other moms upped the ante by bragging how their five-year-old could tabulate a rhombus by multiplying exponents by pi, even though their child was still drinking from a sippy cup. My son wasn't potty trained; his first word was "hurry," and I caught one of my kids eating dirt in the backyard. I fell into a depression, too vulnerable to express my concerns. Instead, I padded myself with isolation, the precise breeding ground for disconnection. The loneliness I felt created a place of solitary confinement.

I fell into isolation when I separated myself from the pack. That separation came from being on a different economic level, comparing myself to others, trusting the wrong people, dealing with different ages and stages, and plain ol' miscommunication. I wasted days and weeks trying to figure out why someone didn't like me until one day I realized it was never about me, to begin with. As Bernard Baruch said, "Don't worry about what others think. Those who mind don't matter, and those who matter don't mind."

As a parent, it's easy to fall into the trap of feeling like you're not enough. We're like transistor radios picking up signals: The way another mom reacted in carpool, a snippy remark by a co-worker, your spouse forgetting an important event, or walking into a room and no one saying, "Hello." All of these signals can make us feel uninvited, rejected, and not enough.

Have you ever asked your husband if your butt was too big? I bet nine times out of ten, it's not about your butt. You're seeking approval, validation. You're seeking affirmation that you're doing a great job, that you're needed and appreciated in your section of the universe. But guess what? Your husband, your friends, that carpool mama, the co-worker—none of them can pull you from the despair. We have to put our eyes on the Maker, the one who designed us so purposefully, who weaved every intricate detail of the fiber of our being.

Instead of believing the truth, we may listen to an unrelenting voice that sounds exactly like our own, telling us we're not enough. In doing so, we're leading our kids and our family down the same path. We're allowing the lie to steal our life. We're allowing thieves to walk through the front door in plain sight, undermining our success and wrecking our future.

Social media has formulated the perfect storm for mom guilt, judgment, and comparison traps. It reflects only the beautiful parts of life, the most perfect angles, the most exotic vacation spots, and the happiest moments. On social media, I, too, had done the very thing I hated in others. My kids made me breakfast in bed for Mother's Day, so of course, I had to document it, or it didn't count. Every corner of my bedroom had a hamper full of dirty clothes and kids' toys. It took somewhere around seven photos to get the best, laundry-free angle—cropped, of course—to post online. I was perpetuating the same fake, idealistic life that made me cringe. No matter where I turned, there were few, if any, discussions of moms struggling with postpartum depression, laughing about their mistakes, posting pictures of destroyed laundry rooms, or applauding others for being just a good mom. So that week, I created my first blog.

It's been my goal to help other moms connect, laugh, relate, discuss, and empower one another through authenticity, vulnerability, and intentional living. I live for those moments when moms realize guilt, perfectionism, and comparison traps are counterfeit options to grace, progress, and contentment when moms recognize that vulnerability doesn't have to be a sign of weakness, but a platform for change. We can't allow such mental distractions to hold us hostage from living our best lives.

Sharing struggles can make you feel raw and vulnerable. My immediate reaction is to cover it quickly—to hide my weakness from the world, conceal it, protect it, tuck it in my carry-on, and lug the weight of my struggle alone. I make it look as though I've got it together when it's exactly the opposite. But this strategy perpetuates the very attitude that created my isolation. We need to be authentic. We need to cheer each other on, like the sisterhood that we are. Let's rally in the tough times and celebrate in the good ones. Choosing your tribe is as essential as selecting who will care for your precious child on date night. Tim Ferriss, author of TOOLS OF TITANS, asserts: "You are the average of the five people you most associate with." Uh oh, who needs new friends? Choosing your people is as vital as appointing who will raise your children in your will. Selecting your team can set you up for success or failure.

Choose your mom tribe wisely. Find those close friends willing to laugh, cry, and celebrate all the moments. Seek out those people willing to protect those fragile pieces too painful to share. Find those willing to pray for you rather than gossip, to take the phone calls at any hour of the day, to be your back up, your go-to, your hoot-and-holler section. These are your people. Your vulnerability is a special place, because when life feels unsolved, stripped, and exposed, it's a platform for change.

You may ask, "But what if I trust my vulnerability to the wrong people? What if I can't find my tribe? What if I end up like you, feeling hopeless and isolated?" It's possible — all of it. But guess what? You won't die. Authentic women are everywhere. If you don't have a great group of girlfriends, stop right now. Whatever you're doing, set it down and find these people. They are the women who make life worth living. I would trade all of my chocolate and a really good box of wine to have these girls in my life. Hear me. They could be in a bookstore, at church, at pre-school, at a football game, at a coffee shop, at a women's conference, on a tennis team, or in a Circle K. Look for them. These women are your lifeline. They create breathing room, security, a safe harbor to laugh, cry, and connect.

I've been lucky enough to find a great group of friends who tell it like it is, who hold me accountable, who cry when I cry, and who laugh until we pee in our pants—and they do it all with great love. We've practically raised each other's kids from pre-school to productive citizens. We've ridden life's rough roads together in the form of G.R.I.T.S. Night (Girls Raised in the South), a quarterly catch-up to discuss life, love, and the pursuit of happiness. One of our quarterly gatherings landed us at Kim's lake house for the weekend. The afternoon started with a laugh session. Someone snorted, and y'all, we could not contain ourselves. It was downhill from there. The ADULTING sign had been turned off, and IMMATURE-ACTING TEENAGERS had taken its place. We were no good for anyone.

By 4 p.m., we found ourselves on a ski boat, flying through the water on inner tubes. It was pure therapy. In the name of safety, Kim handed out red life jackets. For the record, they were the world's smallest ones. She swore they were standard size, but for someone who had just had a baby and was still nursing, I questioned her life-jacket-fitting expertise: "I'm telling you, I grew up on the lake, and Kim, this is a child's life jacket." The snickering, the snorting, and the laughs continued. I had grown from a C cup to a Double D, and the zipper wouldn't budge four inches from the top. The more I zipped, the more stitching began to pop! I jumped into the lake and became my own buoy. My friend Lori, who deserves the gold star for being the sweetest and mature-est of us all, agreed to ride with me on the inner tube. It was time to show off our skills. As the boat jerked forward, Lori and I white-knuckled the ski rope, as we listened to the girls laughing about my chest weighing down the boat and how the engine was having a hard time pulling us. As I thought to myself, OH, I'LL SHOW THEM, out of the blue, just as the boat jumped its first wave, the engine caught on fire!

The girls hollered, and some jumped overboard. There were buckets of water flying around the boat as the smoke billowed higher. The engine was on fire for real fire. The girls were trying to call for help on cell phones with no service, and I questioned whether my boobs actually caused the engine to catch on fire. Kim's boat story has become legend. She claims the life jacket was never the same. The boat didn't survive, but we did—and when we get together, no matter how long it's been, it's like coming home. To this day, Kim, Lori,

Jennifer, Shelly, and Karen are those women who have been my rock through all of life's ups and downs. What is life without connection, without community, without a space for breathing room? Proverbs 18:24 reminds us, "One who has unreliable friends soon comes to ruin, but there is a friend who sticks closer than a brother." I pray you experience such love and support from your tribe. I know it's hard, especially when life changes—a job, a spouse, a home. It's difficult. I've experienced loss. I've moved across the country, leaving friends and family behind, completely starting over from scratch. I now live over two thousand miles from those very women. Starting over can feel lonely, frustrating, and hopeless at times. But like the rising of a Phoenix from the ashes, joy comes in the morning. There will be laughter and good times again. If you've experienced change or loss, or feel uprooted, there's a book that I've placed in my arsenal of must-reads, AFTER THE BOXES ARE UNPACKED by Susan Miller, which reminds us that we can bloom where we are planted.

Find your tribe. Seek them out like a hidden treasure. We are walking past incredible women daily. We just have to reach out and make the connection. Be the first to say "hello" or lend a helping hand. Show up to events, not knowing a soul, and welcome those you don't know. Take them under your wing. Join a Bible study, a running group, or a writers' club. Attend school activities with the kids and connect with other moms. Jump into the land of the living, imperfections and all, and watch change occur.

Choose wisely the tribe you surround yourself with for this is the place that holds your truth and strength. Will you be a member of the Barn-Burning Club or the Hoot-and-Holler Section? List what keeps you on the sidelines of life in isolation and fear. It's time to find your tribe.

Four Ways to Discover Your Tribe

1. What organization, hobby, or group could you join to meet new people?

2. Who could you serve, and where could you serve them?

3. Who is one person you could reach out to? Make a lunch date with them this week.

4. If you could be vulnerable with a friend, what topic would you discuss?

My Prayer

Lord, help me to reach out and find my tribe. Help me to find those women whom I can trust, who can lift me up and encourage me. Help me to encourage myself, be my own dream defender, and believe that because I am fearfully and wonderfully made, I have nothing to prove. I have always been enough. In Your Name, Amen.

CHAPTER 2
IDENTITY THIEF

Beauty begins the moment you decide to be yourself.

~Coco Chanel~

I was wearing yesterday's makeup, and my hair looked like a camel had licked it. It was 6 a.m., and I had just finished an early-morning kickboxing session as the sun began to rise. I needed coffee, stat. As I pulled into the drive-thru, the lady asked for my order. I was so used to speaking my texts instead of typing them that I asked, "Do you have pumpkin spice lattes, *question mark?*" *Did I just say, "question mark?"* I thought. *Oh, dear Lord, perhaps she didn't hear me.* And with a slight giggle, she responded, "Yes we do, *period.*" As I slowly drove towards the window in my eighteen-year-old red

Ford Expedition, a vehicle I use to haul small trees, she asked what my plans were for the day.

I blurted out, "It's a writing day."

"What are you writing?" she asked.

I'm thinking, *Whoa Nelly, that's too many questions before I've had my morning coffee.*

"A book," I said.

"Oh, do tell a book on what?"

As I scanned the smeared windows that looked like a pack of wolves had licked them, I said, "I'm writing a book on living your best life." You should have seen the expression on her face. As I took my coffee and pulled away from the drive-thru, I caught a glimpse of myself in the side-view mirror and couldn't stop laughing. Sometimes in life, we don't look like who we are. Sometimes, we don't look like where we are headed. I knew who I was. The car didn't define me. Neither did the frazzled hair or sticky windows. I'm on a mission to help women discover their superpower, to live in their passion and purpose. And an eighteen-year-old Expedition hauling a small tree would not hold me back. Not today, Satan.

But there are days I wonder, *Who am I?* As my life transitions from one season to another, I'm on a quest of self-discovery. Between the roles we play, the layers of responsibility are compounded, muffling our true self—just being a girl minus all of life's demands. Stripped from the labels we wear, who are we? No one tells you we'll be re-adjusting throughout our lives. With every phase, with each new set of circumstances, with every new chapter, we're constantly re-calculating. What makes us who we are? Our DNA tells us if we'll be left-handed or right-handed. It decides our skin, hair, and eye color. These are the non-negotiables. Then you have your personality—that determines if you are an extravert, an introvert, a peace-maker, an enthusiast, and so on. And finally, you have a superpower, the gift God gave you that makes you unique. The gift of teaching, leading, creating, designing, building, listening, quilting, or organizing. Maybe sales is your niche, and it comes naturally to you. We all have something. If you don't know what your superpower is, ask your friends—they should know.

In life, we are taught early on to please others, to fit in, to not rock the boat or there will be consequences. We're rewarded and applauded for being what other people need. And we're disciplined for being what they don't. So, we begin to please our parents, our teachers, our bosses, our partners, our mother-in-law and the PTA. Perhaps you only had your dad's attention when you were funny—and now, you're an entertainer. A toxic relationship taught you toe the line. You wonder why you're a people pleaser or a perfectionist, trying to create smooth transitions, to steady the waves and control all the things. It's human nature to want to be liked, to want to fit in. Before long, all the voices in our head that direct our steps push out the only voice that matters: our own.

It's important to step back and write down what makes you happy. What makes you brim with delight, giddy for the road ahead? What are your passions, hobbies, and talents? What are your virtues and characteristics? When you wake up to face the day, has your to-do list become a checkbox of *have to*s or *want to*s? Who is driving the boat: intentional living or someone else's agenda? In an effort to figure out my identity, I began to pray and write down what I liked and didn't like. I had never asked my opinion. I was a girl who wasn't bothered by much, and yet some things bothered me greatly. I was simple and complex. I began to think about me and made myself the listener of my own thoughts. A paradigm shift took place in how I viewed the world in how I viewed myself. Those who were disappointed in me for being me decided to walk a different path. I had to let those people go and grieve the loss. I chose to see it as a gift rather than a disappointment. I had won my freedom back to do, to be, to fly.

Want to understand yourself better? Go on a date with you. Take a road trip, swing at the park, or climb a tree. Did you love painting as a kid or running races? Perhaps you were known for being the best listener on the playground, and now you want to be a counselor. There are threads that run through the fabric of our lives, whispering, telling us of our identity, our calling, and our purpose. We have to prepare our hearts to listen to the still small voice within. I took the Enneagram personality test to understand my major and minor personality types better. Are you an achiever, a leader, a thinker, a reformer, a peacemaker, an enthusiast, or a caretaker? Are you an introvert with an achiever personality? Don't deny your DNA. Don't negate your purpose, the reason you were born. You have been placed on this earth to create, design, crunch numbers, love, inspire, encourage, build, console, lead, invent, or compose. Figure out what makes your soul sing and run towards it.

It was a celebratory Sunday evening, the night before I left for college. (Oklahoma or bust!) I found my mom in the living room, rummaging through the suitcase, writing my name on all my belongings. I figured no one would care about my Ferriss Bueller T-shirt, but my mom was on a mission to save it all. During my first week of school, at an all-student prayer service, I walked timidly up to the front row and knelt to pray. Hoping I'd blend into the crowd, I made eye contact with no one. As I turned to stand up, something horrifying caught my eye—on the bottom of each heel, written with a black sharpie, was my full name in all caps, from toe to heel, sixteen letters on each shoe! If embarrassment could kill, I would have died that night. I was lost, but now I'm found. All I had to do was look at my shoes to remember who I was. From that week on, my identity was known by everyone, as complete strangers shouted through the dorm halls, "Hi, Stephanie!" I knew who I was at home, but college pushed me to redefine myself. I would be doing this for the rest of my life.

Life is a perpetual state of transition. Most of us move from high school to college, take our first big paying job as a single person, get married, and purchase our first home. We look around to see what other people are doing, and where they are on their similar paths. We begin to measure our success against their success. We look to our neighbors, their cars, their kids, their schools, and social media as a measuring stick for success. We compare the beginning of our journey to the middle of another's and fall short every time. We look sideways for the answers regarding our worth instead of upwards to the Creator. Ephesians 2:10 tells us, "We are God's masterpiece, created to do good works which God prepared in advance for us to do." Our identity was set in place—from the moment of our creation, Christ redeemed us through the cross. We know who we are and whose we are. There's no need to compare ourselves to others, to determine where we land on the totem pole of life. We are His Workmanship, His Masterpiece. We have our own path, our own personality, and our own identity. We need to stay in our lane and live according to our purpose.

Life was pretty simple, growing up. All I needed was a good bike, a fishing pole, and a trampoline. Brushing my hair wasn't a high priority, but tree climbing was. In hindsight, we lived in a modest home. I had no idea how much money my parents made or what our social status was. To me, life was full of adventure, dirt roads, and bike ramps. I was living my authentic life. Experiences overshadowed material items. When I grew up, got married, and started a family, my husband and I moved to the big city of Atlanta, Georgia. We bought a house that seemed way too big for us. It was full of large windows, high ceilings, and lots of character, precisely decorated to reflect my Southern roots. But then we made a mistake. Over the holidays, we visited a friend's home that was exponentially more fabulous than our own, located on a five-acre farm near the edge of town. Upon arriving home, I scanned my living room and disappointment set in. Suddenly, my ceilings felt too low, the TV seemed too small, the enclosed kitchen felt too tight, and I was pretty sure the living room had shrunk! Instead of staying in my lane and being perfectly satisfied with my identity, my mission and purpose in life, I began to compare; and from that moment on, my contentment meter was broken. There would always be a dangling carrot just beyond my reach.

That experience set me on a quest to attain the golden handcuffs to grasp the brass ring. I lived in a constant state of questioning: when is the house big enough or the corporate title impressive enough? The problem with this pie-in-the-sky mentality was that it had no finish line. There was no racecourse with a flag at the end that told me I had made it ("Congratulations, you are officially successful. You can rest now"). I wrestled with comparison traps, as contentment eluded me at every corner. Contentment is the state of being satisfied. It is a *state*, not an *estate*! The grass was always greener somewhere else. The school I was not accepted to seemed more prestigious. The house I drove by and couldn't afford would make me happier. Life was never quite good enough because I couldn't determine what "good enough" meant.

So, discontentment settled in like a cozy blanket on a crisp day. I gave the very weed I was trying to uproot, the best spot in my garden. My contentment meter was off-kilter. I sought what I couldn't have. I chased what

I didn't need. All to keep up with the status quo. Who was I trying to impress and why?

> Dr. Juliana Breines, author of *The Perils of Comparing Ourselves to Others*, explains,
> *When we compare ourselves to others, we are dividing comparisons into two categories—downward and upward. The downward comparison involves comparing yourself to someone you perceive as worse off than yourself and upward involves comparing yourself to someone you perceive as better off. The comparisons may be based on appearance, health, intelligence, ability, social status, and wealth. Research suggests that we're more likely to make downward comparisons when our self-esteem is threatened.*

Here we are using someone's misfortune to make ourselves look good: what a fragile existence. Comparisons take us above or below someone—never allowing us to partner, side by side, where true strength resides. Comparison creates discord. We can't build team players when comparison is the main ingredient. James 3:16 says, "For wherever there is jealousy and selfish ambition, you will find disorder and every kind of evil." Jealousy and selfish ambition occur when we try to outdo or outrank someone for the sake of eclipsing them. We need to be first, to be perceived as the best. We need to feel accepted, to rank ourselves amongst the herd. Were you the homecoming queen, with the need to perpetuate that image? Are you trying to look like Mom of the Year when you're exactly the opposite? Where does this come from and when does it end?

It's time to weed out what threatens to destroy our garden. Instead of saying, "She is hipper, younger or cooler than me," say, "She is hip." The end. Remove the comparison traps that end in *than me*. Speak truth. Feed your soul with the Word of God: "You will know the truth, and the truth will set you free" (John 8:32). Comparing denies your originality. It denies God's true calling for your life. In the words of Sandra Stanley, author of *Comparison Traps*, "Celebrate what God gave others and leverage what God has given you."

You shouldn't have to prove anything to anyone. Whether you were born under chaotic circumstances, adopted, fostered, conceived by in vitro, planned, or an oopsie-daisy, rest in the fact that God has a purpose and plan for your life. You were created to do great things. You no longer have to struggle, plead, or please to prove your place. On our own, we will always long for more. But with God, we are redeemed. Now, I understand that our goal is to keep our lives free from the *love* of money and be content with what we have, because God has said, "Never will I leave you; never will I forsake you" (Hebrews 13:5). We have God, and He will provide everything we need. So, stop seeking material items to fill a spiritual void. Only God can satisfy you, mend the broken heart, restore the fractured past. Without Him, you'll always be lacking. But through salvation and grace, you will no longer have to strive, prove, or hustle for your worth. Just as those shoes had my name boldly written on them, claiming their owner, your life should proudly proclaim your name, the owner of your life. It's time to discover your true self and write your name on it.

You may ask, "What if I can't stop comparing? What if I reach my goals, and it's not enough? What if people see the real me and don't like it? What if I'm always longing for the next big thing?" Your focus dictates the direction in which you're headed. If you're always looking left or right, you'll end up in the ditch. If your voracious appetite can't be satisfied with a car, a house, money, or things, there will be disappointment at every turn. Paul writes in 1 Timothy 6:6-7, "Godliness with contentment is great gain. For we brought nothing into this world, and we can take nothing out of it." The car, the club membership, the upgraded house will never provide the happiness we seek, because the void we need filled, will never be satisfied with man-made objects. Only Jesus Christ can bring peace, comfort, joy, and redemption. We're looking in the wrong places. Delight in the goodness around you. Journal your gratefulness. Instead of looking inward, serve others. Your attitude will change, and those grey skies will be filled with silver linings.

When sin entered the world through Adam and Eve, a strand of insecurity made us look around instead of up. Galatians 4:4-5 reminds us, "God sent his Son to redeem those under the law, that we might receive adoption to sonship." God sent his Son to redeem us, to compensate for our faults. God bought us with a price, with the cross. We are now living in the royal priesthood—not of our own doing, but simply as a gift from God. How we live, our journey is where the legacy is created. Let's live in grace and contentment, with authenticity and purpose.

We often spend a significant portion of our lives in negative talk. *I don't belong. I should be further along in life. I should be a better cook, wife, mother, daughter.* The struggle is real. We perceive that everyone else is doing life better. Our lives, our kids, our seasons of life are all unique.

"I have learned to be content, whatever the circumstances. I know what it is to be in need, and I know what it is to have plenty. I have learned the secret of being content in any

and every situation, whether well-fed or hungry, whether living in plenty or in want. I can do everything through Christ, who gives me strength" (Philippians 4:11-13).

See, even God reminds us that we have everything we need inside of us. Our identity is in Him; therefore, we don't need to outrank one another to be content. Walk-in your truth, knowing the God who created you, made you for greatness, as the one and only.

So, no more looking side-to-side to see where you rank on the comparison scale. Drop the striving and straining and rest in Him. Live your true self with eyes wide-open, grabbing hold of your identity and, with a Black Sharpie, writing your name on your soul. You compete with no one because God made you an original. You are a mess and a masterpiece—but, sister, I'm here to tell you, you've always been enough.

Four Ways to Discover Your Identity

1. Compose a list of your superpowers, those God-given gifts that make you unique.

2. List attributes of your personality. What are its pros and cons?

3. Identify your favorite activities, your hobbies, your passions.

4. Create a vision board of possibilities. As a child of God, created custom in His image, what have you always dreamed of, but not pursued?

My Prayer

Lord, help me not to compare myself to others but to know that I am an original—that you have placed a passion in my heart, with gifts and talents; that no one can create, say, do or write like me. Help me to seek your wisdom and be a better me today than the me I was yesterday. In Your Name, Amen.

CHAPTER 3
ENDINGS THAT CREATE BEGINNINGS

*The Waiting Place is the special spot on the journey,
to rest, reflect and breathe.*

~Stephanie Pletka~

I *love* new beginnings. I love it when a new door opens, when new friends join my circle, or when a new experience spurs me to go on an adventure. It brings oxygen, a freshness to my life. However, a new beginning means that something else has ended. Each transition has us navigating new territory. When a butterfly extends its beautiful wings, it's no longer a crawling caterpillar. Eventually, a swimming tadpole becomes a frog perched on a lily pad, and such is the circle of life.

Throughout our journey, we will discover new phases and cycles, new seasons, and transitions. We are dynamic creatures—never standing still, but always evolving. I love new beginnings, but endings are tough. There will be a closure, a termination, a finale that perhaps I didn't foresee. Who knew that was the last conversation, the last hug, the last laugh, or the last goodbye?

I have a hard time with endings. Things I enjoyed, whomever I laughed with. There's something about laying that season to rest. It's a death of sorts. On my oldest son's first day of high school, after years of homeschooling four kids, the principal asked all-freshman parents and students to meet in the auditorium to participate in a spirited pep rally. As we said our goodbyes, I made the long walk back to the car empty-handed, not a single child in tow. It was as if someone had snatched my son, literally stole him from me. His life, all the good times—his first word, how he ran to me as a toddler as if I were his only comfort—flew through my mind. I made it to the car before I lost it. We're talking the ugly cry.

Our family of six had the best summer, traveling cross-country, hiking through national parks, laughing, telling stories, sharing wisdom for future trials to come. Oh, to put time in a bottle. Even though our kids can make us crazy, there's something to be said for all the long walks, late-night talks, laughs in the kitchen, and reflection on the porch swing. The stories told, tears cried, hearts broken, and laughs that turn into snorts are priceless moments. And no matter how far they drive you to madness, if anyone messed with them, you would fiercely protect them until the bloody, dirty end, with tear-filled eyes and a full heart. Subtle moments that seem so nonchalant make the lasting impressions.

We raise our kids to leave us (or at least leave the basement) to go into the world to contribute, to throw color and kindness on humanity, to be productive citizens. Our kids are placed in our lives for a season. They are on loan to us. And yet, when the college applications, girlfriends, and boyfriends begin to widen our inner circle, we might see these outsiders as the enemy—the one taking away all those memories and all those moments. Instead of seeing this transition as the end, let us view the end as a new beginning, a new chapter, as an opportunity to increase our love and allow our hearts to grow. It's what makes the world go round, what increases our circles, what allows us to become the butterfly, to grow and thrive. Like Isaiah 43:19 says, "I am doing a new thing; now it springs forth, do you not perceive it? I will make a way in the wilderness and rivers in the desert."

I've never thought of myself as a slow-paced, yoga type of girl, but rather a triathlon racing, tennis-ball-whacking one. So, when I pulled a muscle and had to quit tennis for a while, what seemed like a bleak season of life turned out to be the best. I should have let the tennis door close naturally. I hopped and hobbled, hoping to play a little longer. The Southern girl in me fought tooth and nail when I should have graciously let it go, waiting for what was behind Door Number Two.

They say a true lady knows when to leave, a lesson hard learned. I loved tennis. It was free therapy. It kept me fit and provided me with a social outlet. It was my way into all my girls' luncheons, weekend parties, girls' nights out. It was good for my soul. But my favorite exercise, chasing a yellow ball, had ceased to exist in my reality. So now what? I joined a gym and looked at the exercise class schedule to see what class worked best for me—yoga. Ugh! I'm probably the least coordinated, Zen-loving, slow-pace-hating, leg-contorting, dirty-dog-posing girl you'll ever meet. What could I possibly get out of a yoga class?

Upon my husband's slight nudge, I signed up for this adventure, which was clearly outside my comfort zone. I didn't have a mat, I wasn't flexible, and I felt claustrophobic in dark spaces. I walked into the class, and a perky, pig-tailed instructor sauntered up to me and said, "We're so glad you came today. Wherever you are is where you are supposed to be." This hit me like a ton of bricks. *Wherever I am is where I'm supposed to be?* Had she been watching the story of my life through a hidden camera? Perhaps the tennis door closed so that I could hear those words. It rocked me to the core. The mama in me comes from the school of, *Wherever I am, I should be somewhere else. Whatever I am, I should be someone else. Whoever I am, is not enough.*

Maybe tennis wasn't the end-all, be-all. Maybe a door had closed for another to open. This, perhaps, wasn't an accident. I wouldn't have taken this class if the tennis door had not been closed, locked, and boarded up because I had a crowbar, and I wasn't scared to use it. As I began to hold stances that would make a grown man cry—while sweating, screaming inside, trying to figure out how to escape through the side door—I found a peace I hadn't felt in years.

The next week I enrolled in my first meditation class—and wouldn't you know, I was the only one who signed up. Y'all, I needed to blend in, not stand out. The instructor said, "Raise your hand if you've never taken a meditation class." I slowly looked around the empty room and raised my hand. Awkward. With candles flickering along the wall, we both sat Indian style. "Close your eyes, and just breathe." I kept opening one eye to see what was happening. My internal dialogue whispered, *Dear Lord, Stephanie, close your eyes. The woman is not going to steal your flip-flops.* It was too quiet. Oh goodness, I was certain the instructor could hear my stomach growling (having eaten only two blueberries as I'd rushed out of my house). She clanged a chime and meditation began.

"Breathe deep and relax your forehead," she said.

I didn't realize my forehead needed relaxing, but it did.

"Relax your ears."

Who knew that was a thing? But it was.

"Drop your shoulders."

Mine were still perched in fight-or-flight mode.

"Clear your mind of all thoughts."

I couldn't stop thinking.

"If your thoughts become active, guide them back to your center."

I need to get the oil changed in my car.

I bet the kids have torn up the house.

Uh-oh, start reeling in your thoughts.

Wait, did she say to guide my thoughts, or reel them in. Oh crap, which is it?

Quit thinking.

Stop thinking about thinking.

Are my ears still relaxed? I don't know.

Who knew doing nothing took so much work?

As I finally began to relax my ears, rest my mind, lower my shoulders and breathe, all the sounds of guests walking down the hall in full conversations dissipated. Fifty minutes felt like fifteen. As she rang the end-of-session chime, it sounded much louder than before. There was a prolonged silence, like a waiting place. Instead of popping out of a meditative state, she eased me out with a quiet reminder to be thankful and to walk in gratitude as I made decisions throughout the day. This concept of a waiting place to sit in during a transition has changed my life. For many of us, the waiting place often feels like a holding pattern. Perhaps we think it's wasted time with a fruitless purpose, but it actually holds a significant transition in our season of life. It's where we rest, relax, refuel, and hear God's voice. It's where we obtain our second wind, re-strategize, and move forward with purpose. Have you ever driven across the country without taking a break or without a rest stop to fuel? It's not a good idea. You'll end up on the side of the road, stranded, with hungry kids. The same is true with us if we don't take time to breathe, relax, and rest.

The Waiting Place is the space between an ending and a beginning. It is a rest stop during a transition that allows us to be still, to be mindful, to bring awareness and acceptance to the moment. Strategic rest stops allow quick tempers to give way to patience, and anger to shift to kindness. Rest stops changed the way I thought about breathing, the way I listened to the rustling of the wind, the way I got out of bed each morning, and how I responded to others throughout the day. It provides a moment of respite to appreciate my gifts and to give thanks. It's amazing what can happen when we remove ourselves from the distractions of life and rest in His presence.

When I truly sit in the hard moments to find the lesson, it helps me build strength and stamina, empowering me for the road ahead. As I embraced what each season wanted to teach me, I began to let go of self-imposed baggage. In my turmoil, I found peace in His refuge: "He who dwells in the secret place of the Most High shall abide under the shadow of the Almighty. I will say of the Lord; He is my refuge and my fortress. My God in Him, I will trust" (Psalm 91:1-2). The blessings come when I remove myself from life's turbulence, knowing that wherever I am is where I am supposed to be.

Perhaps your child is dealing with health issues, and your situation seems relentless. Maybe you're running from an unsalvageable marriage or trying to extend a temporary friendship not meant for long-term use. Perhaps you're in a job you can't fathom waking up to for another six months, or you're dealing with family issues that will never be resolved. Maybe you've dwelled on past hurts that only God can redeem. Are you trying to pry open a door that is meant to be closed? Are you trying to walk through a door that's not ready to be opened? There's a process, a lesson God is bestowing on us, in various seasons of life. If we dart through them, I fear the seasons will need repeating. In order to learn the lesson, in order to hear the message, in order to have metamorphosis, one needs the elements of heat and time. When life heats up, it's easier to run. But the journey creates the transformation. It's where iron sharpens iron. It's where you fall and get back up. It's where mental toughness and muscle memory remind you how far you've come. This is where a caterpillar becomes a butterfly and coal becomes a diamond. It's where beauty is formed from the ashes.

What if you're living in a place that doesn't feel like home? What if you're bucking the system at every stop along the way? Don't skip the transition just because it feels uncomfortable. If you can't sit in the moment, live in the present, and bloom where you're planted, your bucket will be full of despair, heartache, and frustration. You may be in a predicament that makes your skin crawl. Life has heated up, and you're ready to bolt. Pray and ask God to show you the lesson. New doors have a way of opening when the lesson has been learned. Perhaps your spouse lost a job, and you feel angry that you've had to downsize your life. This unexpected diversion was not on your original road map. Instead of being angry and resentful, use this transition to show grace, mercy, and understanding.

Joseph, a young shepherd, was sold into slavery by his jealous brothers. He felt forgotten by his family (and, for a time, by God). Little did he know, he was in the Waiting Place, the spot where good things happen—where patience is tried, lessons are learned, and skills are honed. Joseph's experience got him appointed to one of the most powerful positions in the land, only second to the King. His sufferings made way for his gifts. It created the relationships and formed the fabric that would tell a greater story of forgiveness, redemption, love, and provision. The Waiting Place taught Joseph what he needed for the road ahead. If he lacked patience to push through this season, he might have missed God's calling. What season of life are you trying to hurry through? What doors are you trying to pry open that aren't ripe for the taking? Put away the crowbar and allow God to do His great work. Walk through open doors and step away from the closed ones. Find the fire and allow it to teach you. God has a plan to give you a future and a hope (Jeremiah 29:11). He knew you before the world began and created you in His perfect image. So, walk in faith, knowing that where you are is where you are supposed to be.

Four Ways to Thrive in Your Season of Life

1. Write down a time you relied on God to open or close a door.

2. Name ways you can adapt to change during various seasons of life.

3. List two ways you can be optimistic when a door is closing.

4. Describe three ways to bloom where you are planted.

My Prayer

Lord, help me not to rush through seasons that feel uncomfortable. Help me to savor all the moments. Help me to learn what I'm supposed to take away from each phase of life and always appreciate that where I am is where I am supposed to be. In Your Name, Amen.

CHAPTER 4

THE PATH TO SELF-DISCOVERY

You will know the truth and the truth will set you free.

~John 8:32~

Swim, bike, run! I hadn't raced in a triathlon since I was in my mid-twenties. My *Swim, bike, the run* had become *carpool, laundry, and shepherding teen hearts.* A few things have changed over the years: my weight and fitness level. My attention had been placed on the kids. I decided to reverse the trend and focus on me. At first, it felt selfish. I gave all the excuses in the world. But ultimately, my husband encouraged me to walk towards my path of self-discovery. Step One: Join a gym. Check! My ultimate goal was to swim fourteen laps at my local pool. That didn't seem difficult until

I began swimming. Four laps in, I felt like I couldn't catch my breath. It was way more cardio-intensive than I remembered. My heart felt as if it would burst. My body didn't seem to glide through the water as it once did. A lifeguard came running towards me, waving her arms. Alarmed, I stopped. Was someone hurt? Was I in the wrong lane? She said, "Ma'am, are you ok?" My mind went blank. Did she say, *ma'am*? "You seem to have difficulty swimming. If you need assistance, there are floaties in the closet." Floaties? Was she talking to me? I responded. "Oh, I'm training for a triathlon." She giggled. "They're in the closet if you need them." Y'all, I couldn't even. The lifeguard thinking, I needed floaties was all I could dwell on.

I could still remember my old swim cap color: it was yellow, a megaphone to the world that I was young. This time, when the race official wrote my age on the back of my leg with a Sharpie, I wanted to explain, *I actually feel younger than this!* Now, I no longer wore a yellow cap, reserved for the twenty-somethings, but a purple one, for those in their forties. To make matters worse, our age category placed us second-to-last to enter the water. The racers I feared most, the quick-as-lightning twelve-to-eighteen-year olds, were waiting in the wings to surpass us at Mach speed. I prayed, *Please, God, don't let me end up in last place.* Surely, there was one slower soul who didn't train as much as I did. *Let this be their consequence, Lord, not mine.*

All along the race of life, we are apologizing for our age, our personality, or our need for floaties. Don't apologize for who you were yesterday or who you are becoming today. No one said it would be easy. Run the race, sister. All of these processes are taking you one step closer to being you, your true, no-holds-barred, authentic self.

Embrace the wisdom you've gained in the years you've lived: "Let us run with endurance the race God has set before us" (Hebrews 12:1). Wave your purple swim cap proudly. Like the markings on your leg, all things mature, and with development comes freedom and adventure. Embrace who you are, every step of the way.

Growing up, I was quite an active child: a running, tumbling, flipping, cartwheeling, energetic kind of girl. You might even say I had ADHD on top of my ADHD—Oh look, a quarter! I digress — my poor parents. I was so skinny. I acquired the nickname "Bird Legs" in Fifth Grade. I couldn't gain weight to save myself. My parents took me to the doctor straight from the bus stop, with bags packed, convinced I would be checked into the local hospital for having worms. (Throw that in the counseling bin.) I would flip and roll through the house from one end to the other. I was non-stop. No one ever knew how I would enter or exit a room, but they knew I'd do it quickly.

Now fast forward to adulthood, and I can gain weight smelling a Snickers bar. And then I had my first child. What happened to this body, the one that could lose five pounds just by skipping lunch? If only I were as fat as the last time, I *thought* I was fat. Oh, how I took it for granted when I could wear a two-piece with cut-off jeans, strutting around Walmart, feeling proud. A few weeks after having my first child, our cable TV remote broke and needed to be exchanged. I hopped into the car, grabbing diapers and strollers as if I were moving across country, and away we drove to the cable store. The office was in a heavily wooded area, through a peaceful park-like drive in a corporate district. I arrived early (something that hasn't happened since) waiting for the doors to open. With a little time on my hands,

I noticed my backside in the world's largest mirror. It was an executive building framed in mirrored glass. Waiting for the doors to unlock, I took a quick peek while slowly pushing the stroller, giving myself a critical glance at who I had become. *I wonder what my butt looks like*, I thought. I subtly turned around to make sure no one was looking, and then I gave myself a quick glance off the reflection of the building. With a few looks of disgust, a couple of eye rolls, I looked again to assure my eyes hadn't deceived me. As I squeezed a little butt cheek fat for the second time, a female executive quickly rushed through the front door in a hurried, yet giggling sort of way. "Ma'am," she said, "There's a meeting in Room 101, and nine people have been watching you check out your backside."

"What?" I replied. I was horrified! If that wasn't bad enough, I could hear the roar of laughter as they viewed my reaction. There I was, judging and evaluating my body, and now I was humiliated by a group of executives that I had entertained in a corporate meeting. I surely burned calories pushing the stroller to the car in record time.

I've learned to exonerate myself from such scrutiny. A person can't have a baby and look the same. Motherhood happens. The processes you've been through makes you better, stronger, and wiser. Yes, there are days I wished I had appreciated the times I was more energetic, wishing I was as fat as the last time I thought I was fat. However, it's important to give yourself grace. It's not what you deserve; rather, it's a gift.

Love who you are at whatever size, fitness, or energy level. Celebrate you. There are seasons of life when you'll be on the ground, mending, loving, teaching, and counseling your child. Other seasons will provide more "you" time. Love yourself through it all. Give yourself time to make a comeback. Whatever goal this may be for you, love yourself during the tough times. Be a true friend to you. This will also prove to be a great example to your children as well, allowing yourself grace and cutting yourself some slack. So, the next time you see the world's largest mirror, just smile and keep walking. Don't apologize for being the human that you are. The greatest gift you can provide yourself is allowing you to be you.

I found myself struggling to be me. I wanted to please, to conform. I had trouble cutting ties with those who made me feel small. I lacked the fortitude to hold my ground when they overstepped my boundaries. I felt bad for wanting something different. I felt wrong when they didn't approve. But the drive to chase what I was meant for burned within, like a calling. I began to dream of greater possibilities for my life, but it rocked the boat of certain relationships. They felt threatened by the change. And those who didn't agree with my pursuits gave ultimatums to cut me off, to walk away from the relationship. And it scared me.

I'm a recovering people-pleaser. I had anxiety born from trying to make those around me happy. I was a girl filled with hopes and dreams, beating life to a different drum—and people didn't like it. Those around me tried to contain it to make themselves feel more comfortable. And when I colored outside the lines, I was punished for being different. I began to apologize for just being me. I felt depressed, isolated, wrong, like a bad seed. But the God who made me the way I am made me that way for a reason. And not everyone will understand. And that's okay. It's not our job to explain. It's our job to be ourselves and live our authentic lives. Our entire lives, we will be on a journey of self-discovery. I'm not the same girl I was in elementary school or high school or the girl who married that guy she met on a bus all those years ago. I've traveled many miles along life's path, and each experience has sharpened me. With each new bend in the road, how would I protect the girl who's always becoming?

I began to put parameters in place to protect the life I was building. Instead of coming along for the ride to experience my transformation, those who only wanted me for what they needed—instead of for who I was—punished me in the form of silent treatment or blocking me on social media. I felt like a bad seed. And a couple of times I dropped my pursuits to conform to what they needed me to be, but my heart longed for a different path, and I could not stop walking towards the light.

Dr. Henry Cloud, author of *Necessary Endings*, reminds us: "Without the ability to end things, people stay stuck, never becoming who they are meant to be, never accomplishing what their talents and abilities could afford them. Pruning is a necessity in trimming the sick and dead branches, for the plant to thrive. It's part of the cycle of life." I said yes to things when I should have said no. I did it to please others. I had to remind myself that the backing-out process wouldn't be easy. We all have a role to play. When I said yes, those who overstepped my boundaries flocked to the opportunity. It wasn't their fault that I was in this position. It was my own. A boundary is defined as a limit, as a property line, and without them, you'll find yourself frustrated. Ever notice how sweet a person can be when you say yes to their request? It's like seeing a little girl skipping through the meadow; however, the minute you say no, it's like a scratch on a record. Pandemonium ensues, like a tornado on aisle nine. If you think this behavior is reserved for only children under three-foot-nine, you're mistaken. A true friend will hear the word *no* and respect it.

You'll find that people want to rid themselves of responsibilities, so they are constantly passing the buck like a game of Hot Potato. If you catch the potato, you may get burned, and the potato-thrower will be nowhere in sight. Perhaps a classroom mom tosses you the Christmas party in November, or a family member ties your approval to a behavior. You've watered and fertilized those around you, and now your own root system has begun to die. The beautiful sunflower you once were is barely recognizable.

No is a complete sentence. You don't have to follow it up with other excuses. Just say, "No." With a smile, leave it at that. You owe no one an apology or long-winded reason for your answer. Besides, manipulators will work around your reason. They'll move heaven and earth to give you the opportunity to say yes or to coerce you to say yes. Let peace be your guide. When your gut says no, but your mouth says yes, don't justify that it's for a good cause. Your priority is to your family; all else comes second. I've never met a mom whose to-do list wasn't a scroll. We're not lacking for activities. Decipher why you apologize, why you please, why you deny the Power of You. Find a good counselor, pray, and read scripture to renew your mind. Creating a different lens will initiate a different response, a different view: much like the turning of a kaleidoscope that offers brilliant images with each click. We teach others how to treat us. Our mannerisms, our self-talk, our actions create our journey, which determines our destiny. Throw the hot potato back and stop apologizing. It's time to embrace your true you.

I determine my future. If I fail, I will try again. If I fall, I will get back up. James 12:4 says, "Count it all joy, when you meet trials of various kinds, for you know that the testing of your faith produces steadfastness, that you may be perfect and complete, lacking in nothing." Anything worth having is worth fighting for. The pushing and pulling of adversity equips you for what's ahead. The hardships, the tough times, the falling and getting back up, create physical and mental toughness.

Lysa TerKeurst, the author of *The Best Yes*, says, "A woman who lives with the steps of an overwhelmed schedule will often ache with the sadness of an underwhelmed soul." It's time to draw a line in the sand. Henry Cloud, the author of *Boundaries*, defines boundaries as a property line, determining who is responsible for certain things: "When a boundary is overstepped," he writes, "one becomes a trespasser." Be responsible for what you can control: your feelings, attitudes, choices, and behaviors. When we each take responsibility for our own stuff and stay in our lane, it's the first step to becoming authentic. Remember, not everyone will like you, and that's okay. You don't like everyone, either. You may be too much for one person and not enough for another. That's their problem, not yours. Tyler Perry's character Madea, in the "Tree Speech," reminds us: "Some people come into our life as leaves on a tree, here for only a season. You can't depend on them for anything more than shade. The wind blows, and they are gone." Let's not ask anyone to be anything other than what they are. Instead of denying our differences, let's celebrate them. There are many fish in the sea. You'll find your people, your niche, your groove. Just keep swimming.

Are you tired of handing your power to those with shrouded intentions, whose real goal is to hold you captive from yourself? Don't give the wounded authority over your life. Others can only take the power you give them. Don't sit in the pain that others have bestowed, waiting for relief that may never come. Five, ten, thirty years may have gone by, and you think that someone owes you an apology before you can move forward. Perhaps they've long passed, and you sit in a mental prison, holding the keys to freedom in your hand. Instead of blaming our parents, a boss, or our past, let's pretend the statute of limitations has expired, and no one else is left to blame but ourselves, for what we didn't become.

It's time to establish boundaries and protect the fort. Cloud tells us, "Clear parameters create defined expectations. Defined lines empower you to roam freely in your own space." Don't apologize for your personality, your gifts, or your dreams. Don't deny your soul who it's meant to be. Don't negate your genetic make-up. Don't tarnish your shine to accommodate another. Take those differences and leverage them. Don't allow others to clip your wings. Take ownership of who you are — stand firm in your freedom. You're a gift. The world needs what you have to offer. The world needs you the way you were created. Lift those wings girls, and fly!

What if I establish boundaries and make others mad? What if they don't like me? Well, the chance is high, but it's certainly worth the risk to save your family, your health, and your life. It's time to unload the baggage and hand it all back to their owners: *Here's your briefcase. Here's your purse. Excuse me, here's your stuff.* Little by little, your shoulders will lighten, your back will straighten, and guess what? People won't like it. Sometimes you have to unload the boat to keep it from sinking. Sometimes you have to cut ties to keep from drowning. In the beginning, God created boundaries. He gave Adam and Eve free rein to eat anything from the Garden of Eden . . . Except from the Tree of the

Knowledge of Good and Evil. God made it clear which tree was forbidden. When they ate it, they overstepped their boundary, becoming immediate trespassers. They were banished from the garden where sin entered, and chaos ensued. Boundaries were set, and the consequences were clear. The power of being you needs parameters. My boundaries weren't created to offend others, but to honor me. Guard you. If they don't follow the rules, they have to play elsewhere.

So, no more apologizing for being you. No more denying your soul the identity it's meant to have. The psalmist says in Psalm 139:14, "I praise you Lord, for I am fearfully and wonderfully made. How amazing are your works, for my soul knows it well." God made you in His perfect image; how you're meant to shine, create, love, and make your mark. How do you set up parameters to ensure you are living your best life?

Four Steps to Your Path of Self-Discovery

1. What boundaries must you create to assure others' expectations don't overwhelm you?

2. List three ways to be fearless in your own skin.

3. Who do you blame/what excuses do you tell yourself for not being who God has called you to be?

4. How can you take ownership of your future?

My Prayer

Lord, help me see that You created me in Your perfect image. I have no reason to ever apologize for being anything other than me. Help me to run my race with purpose and freedom, knowing that I am exactly what You had in mind. In Your Name, Amen.

TRANSITION 2
GROWING

CHAPTER 5

CREATE BREATHING ROOM

Slow down. Take a breath. What's the hurry?

-Jeremiah 2:25-

One day I received a call I'll never forget. It started with me lying in bed fifteen minutes longer than usual, having hit the snooze button one time too many. I was pregnant with Baby Number Four and had pulled a late night at work. My body couldn't take another step. My husband's job had him traveling to India for four weeks, and the responsibility of caring for three littles had taken its toll on me. I felt exhausted and hurried. The more I ran late, the *more* I ran late. My life was firing on all four cylinders in a perpetual state of disarray. After dropping off two toddlers at pre-school, I received a call from the teacher.

"We need to talk," she said.

"Were my boys hurt? Is everything ok?" I asked.

"All is well, but I'm worried about you."

"Me?"

How did she know me, my situation, my story? What concerned her enough to have a conversation? Without judgment, she noticed I was consistently frazzled at drop-off. I had paid late fees almost daily at pick-up for skidding into carpool fifteen minutes late, and that was the least of my worries. I was negotiating the sale of my business to be a stay-at-home mom, and I was about to turn into a pumpkin (minus the glass slippers). I couldn't help but cry. I needed someone to notice and reel me back to safety. The chaos of my life was whirling out of control, like a rogue spin top. I needed to create a space for breathing room.

I had created my own marketing brand, my own public relations campaign, and it wasn't pretty. We all have a perception that we've created of ourselves, whether directly or indirectly. People see us as the one who's always late, the exhausted mama, the drama queen, the adventurer, the traveler, the editor, the entrepreneur, the one with all the kids, the mom with the best snacks, the one who's always put together, or the one who never goes anywhere because they have a dog. We know these people. We may *be* these people. We brand ourselves as a leader, efficient, a know-it-all, the mom who makes everything look easy, the fighter, the survivor, the pleaser. We all create our own marketing package. What is yours? Mine had *exhaustion* written all over it.

As humans, we create our own marketing message as to how we present ourselves to the world. Are you your own little entity of perfection, exhaustion, tardiness, or hurriedness? Do you know someone who seems to have the Midas Touch? They probably generate their own success by creating opportunities. Those who dwell in drama often create it via gossip and discord. We've all been there, haven't we ladies? We know someone who's late to every meeting, lunch date, and playgroup, arriving precisely at 12:15 p.m. for a noon appointment. We all have the same 86,400 seconds in a day to spend, yet they always seem to be running a deficit. What does your marketing package say about you? Do words like *disarray, complicated, busy, overload, drained* or *weary* describe you, and therefore your brand? It's time to look inward and figure out what has created this turmoil within us. It's time to rip off the band-aid, decipher the situation, and determine a path to healing. We've become everyone's someone. We want to be known as the breadwinner or the problem solver. We equate busyness with importance, with productivity. But perhaps the busyness of life is a cover-up for something more threatening. Could this be true for you? What are you running from?

Do you compete with others at every turn, trying to prove your existence or your worth? Are you always reaching for the unreachable? Are you an overachiever? I've felt this way, trying to prove my worth, the reason I exist in the universe. I've read tons of self-help books to fix what seems unfixable. Can you relate? You fear to look inward, so you run. You keep swimming; you keep moving—creating the chaos as a distraction, eating your way through an emotional mess. Stop this minute and deal with it. The emotional baggage you carry is affecting your entire world. Instead, "Cast your burdens on the Lord, and He shall sustain you. He will never permit the righteous to be moved" (Psalms 55:22). Procrastination, perfection, and busyness stem from a root cause.

Put a name on it and do the repair work. It's time to slow down. Stop what you're doing and write down what's causing the crazy. Decipher what's creating the chaos. You need breathing room, a little margin, a little grace. It's time to create life's slow-down moments to establish a deeper meaning and purpose, providing community and connection. It's time to savor the goodness. No more bulldozing your way to perfection. No more being late to every event. No more carrying baggage not meant for you to bear — no more going through the motions without feeling all the feels. No one will care about you more than you, and if you allow yourself to be last place, sister, where's the hope? You need to rescue *you*. You need to be your own advocate, your own dream defender. You can only help others if you take care of yourself first.

Have you ever seen a life coach show up to a meeting bone-weary like they don't have their life together? You're thinking, *Uh-oh, I chose the wrong coach.* Don't be this person to your kids or your co-workers. How you represent yourself to the world is your calling card. I'm not talking about the days you wake up with the baby at 3 a.m. There's a season for everything, and some periods need more attention than others. I'm talking about the generalization of you being late or punctual, a gossiper or an encourager, cynical or positive, hurried or calm, wounded, or a warrior. You have the power to create chaos or space. It's in your hands. You are the VP of your public relations brand. You have the ability to establish margin, the space between staying in your own lane and driving off the cliff. Remember the one time you woke up early, ran two miles, drank a protein shake, and washed laundry by 8 a.m.? Winning! You felt on top of the world. When you own the morning, you own the day.

Now, think of those days filled with panic, as you rush out the door with tires squealing. Which one felt better? You get to choose how the day looks. You set the tone. It's not just about doing all the things, but doing them with grace. Get up a little earlier. Prepare the night before. Your job is so much bigger than the job. You're teaching the kids how to handle life. It's not just about the *do*ing: it's about the *be*ing. It's about preparing ahead of time to ensure a positive experience. It's about showing up and giving your best. It's about offering grace in the tough times. Give yourself space to breathe, to take it all in. What is life worth if you can't enjoy the moments? Give yourself space to fail, to learn, to cultivate, to be intentional.

I need quiet time (in the form of journaling and meditation) to prepare for the day, to hold negative thoughts at bay. I need to exercise before the sun rises, padding fifteen extra minutes for bad traffic or a last-minute outfit change. There will be unexpected interjections throughout the day. It's life. A kid will leave their left shoe by the mailbox. There will be a traffic jam on the 101. I'll hit the snooze button one time too many. An unexpected bill will drain the budget. To deal with these issues, preparation is key. Laying out the kid's clothes, making lunches the night before, was a game-changer for me. Saying no to non-essentials is a must. Automating and delegating were also turning points, like online bill pay or grocery store pickup. It feels good to be ahead of the game, carving space to relax, to enjoy the goodness of my life.

Write down a vision for how you want your life to look—"Where there is no vision, people perish" (Proverbs 29:18). Speak life over your thoughts. Like an architect designing house plans, I had to intentionally write down how to create margin in my life. If I wanted breathing room, I needed to carve out space to breathe, rather than relying on my adrenal glands to pump out the last bit of juice to reach my destination. I had to re-train my kids not to rush me with a flurry of last-minute tasks. I had to train them to be independent, to seek their own answers first. This made them more strategic, responsible forward thinkers. The chaos was held at bay and replaced with a more peaceful atmosphere. Instead of creating a marketing package that "the Pletkas are always late, chaotic and hurried," we began to create margin by holding Sunday night meetings to figure out who was responsible for what chores. Upcoming events were placed on a central calendar, and clothes were laid out the night before. Procrastination took a back seat and gave us breathing room to enjoy the goodness of the journey. Listen, mamas: we may live in the crazy *briefly*, but we don't have to reside there permanently. We get to say how this plays out. We can swirl in panic or nest in peace. I choose the latter. Of course, there are days. We're not perfect people by a long shot. If you see us fighting in the church parking lot, please don't judge. We're just regular people. But day by day, moment by moment, we are closer to the breathing room door than the chaotic one.

My father-in-law has found the secret sauce to creating life's slow-down moments: through community and connection. He is a legend in his neck of the woods. Aside from being the town postman, he owns a shooting range and serves on the city water board. He's a fixture in the community, and there's nothing like sitting around a crackling bonfire on a cool summer evening with good whiskey and friends to see how he shines as an incredible storyteller. I only need to say the name Jeff, and people know exactly who I'm referring to. His birthday parties are epic. People come far and wide to celebrate this man. But his relationships did not occur by happenstance. He's cultivated a welcoming atmosphere. Once people meet Grandpa Jeff, they are never a stranger. He's established an after-work environment that allows one's soul to breathe, to marinate in the delight of life. Rushed souls may enter, but it's the restful one who leaves. He'll sit for hours and teach the grandkids hunting safety skills—and later, play a melancholy tune on the guitar as a way to reflect on the day. He's surrounded himself with good quality friends who meet weekly, and because of this, his life is happier, fuller, and more connected than most. He's created life's slow-down button, filled with friendships, connection, and breathing room. Grandpa Jeff inspires me.

The atmosphere you create will determine your legacy. Kids may not remember what you said, but they'll remember how you made them feel. Were they late to every event, with a frazzled mom hanging on by a thread, or did you create tranquility, providing laughter and love along the way? There will be moments we are late, exhausted, and skidding into ballet practice on a wing and a prayer, but they shouldn't be *all* the moments. Take the power back. Don't be a slave to time, finances, or people. Set boundaries create your own rules. Just remember, you're not alone. There are many just like you. I see you, the one staying up late to wash the dishes or feed the baby. I see you, the one who's trying to keep it together when life feels unruly. I see you, the mom who wants her teen to like her, but opts to shepherd their heart instead. Being a mom makes you a member of an incredible club. Find room to breathe, room to connect. While it feels like you are the only one, remember we're all out there in the late hours of the night and wee hours of the morning, pushing through. You are not alone. "There is nothing new under the sun," Ecclesiastes 1:9 says. "What has been will be again; what has been done will be done again." You may be unique, but your circumstances are not. We are in this together.

What if I don't slow down? You may wonder. *What if I continue to procrastinate and live in a constant state of hurriedness and exhaustion? What if I don't create breathing room for friendship and connection?* Then you'll miss it all. Don't live a life of regret. The goodness is sitting before you, in the form of your family, who come home from the chaos of their day to enjoy the peace, security, and restfulness of the environment you've created.

God established the Sabbath as breathing room. He made this commandment a priority. Take one day for yourself. God wants us to sideline our lives from the turbulence. Breathing room affords us a place of rest, to re-strategize, and regroup. You were made to thrive, to dream, to create, and connect. No more burning the candle at both ends. We create our own marketing message as to how we present ourselves to the world, as the exhausted mom paying carpool late fees or living it with arms open wide, padded with connections, guard rails and breathing room. What does your marketing package say about you?

Four Ideas to Create Breathing Room

1. What can you do the night before to prepare for the week ahead?

2. Name two bad habits that keep you from owning the morning.

3. What tools or apps can you download to create a more efficient life?

4. Who or what can you say no to this week to pad your life with a little more margin?

My Prayer

Lord, help me to find ways to slow down my life, to take moments to breathe in the goodness. Thank you for my family, for guardrails, and for protecting me from the hurriedness and chaos that steal the joy of living. I give you glory and praise for my wonderful friends, mentors, and connections that hold me accountable, knowing that my life is not just about the doing, but more about the *be*ing. In Your Name, Amen.

CHAPTER 6
SEX, LIES, AND THE ROLES WE PLAY

*Make it your goal to create a marriage
that feels like the safest place on earth.*

~Gary Smalley~

When John and I first got married, our new love was exciting and intoxicating. We floated to the grocery store, dated, and dreamed together. We didn't come up for air the first year. There were no kids or complicated schedules. We were two lovebirds living in Texas. One evening, I arrived home from work a few minutes earlier than usual, so I decided to surprise him. I planned to greet him in the living room, wearing only a strand of Christmas lights. I have no idea where this notion came from, but I quickly found myself digging through the holiday decorations. Oh, the joys of being married to me. Talk about putting the lights to good use during the off-season. Perhaps I had minutes or an hour to spare. I'm sure if he had a clue, neither traffic nor a late meeting could have detoured him. Not knowing when he would walk through the front door, I began throwing and slinging, running and wrapping as fast as possible. A slow, tedious hour passed. (Isn't that the way it is when you're wrapped in Christmas lights?) The ticking of the clock seemed eternal. Y'all, it didn't occur to me to leave the lights unplugged until the moment he arrived. No, no, this stubborn Alabama girl couldn't make any right decisions until she made all the wrong ones.

Suddenly, he walked through the front door, curious as to what I had up my sleeve. But on this day, I wasn't wearing any sleeves. It was just me in all my glory, tangled up in Christmas lights, with the Star of David in the wrong place at the wrong time, as the heat from tiny bulbs quickly intensified. By the time he walked into the foyer, I had a full-blown Feliz Navidad attack, wrestling with three yards of hot strings that had practically caught on fire. In my desperation to unwind what had caused third-degree burns, I looked like a cat wrestling its own shadow. He fell to his knees in the foyer, laughing, crawling my way to assist in the tangled debacle. My Steady-Eddy, calm engineer husband, who takes everything in stride, whose emotional meter is not swayed by highs or lows, was on the ground, laughing uncontrollably, as he deciphered my predicament.

We look back at those days with laughter and wonder. I sometimes reflect, *Where did this girl go?*—the audacious, fearless, adventurous spirit with a youthful mentality who loved to spark the fire and fan the flame. Well, it's called "kids," "a career," "mortgage," and "bills." It's called "carpool" and "projects," "dinner" and "laundry." As women, we wear many hats. When these roles are new, there's an excitement about it. Those first times are priceless: the incredible smell of your newborn when you hold them for the first time or the first moment you drop your child off at kindergarten or college, as you both venture into new chapters. Oh, the firsts. They're so exciting and new, full of possibilities and potential. Then, life takes a hard turn somewhere at the intersection of Have To and Don't Want To. All those creative dinners with a toast of wine become nightly duties of how many ways to cook a chicken. Then there's the sadness you feel when you realize those kids who graduated won't be coming home as often. You recognize you've exchanged enticing lingerie for a holey pair of cotton comfort that couldn't attract a moth to a light in a dark room. Your husband's abs are long gone as he manages the stress of working sixty-hour work weeks. Life no longer feels wonderful and glamorous.

Just as you're wearing the ugliest (yet most comfortable) jammies known to man, you bend over to scrub something brown off the wall that could equally be chocolate or poo, and your husband slowly walks by and nonchalantly swipes his boner on your back. I mean, really! Are you *kidding* me right now? That's when the Mama, whose job is to be responsible—the juggler of all things, the captain of the ship, the hub to all the spokes—wants to turn around and smack him. We see it as one more item on the to-do list. He's ready for it, willing to take a chance, in case tonight is his night. What if we saw ourselves through his eyes? He sees a sexy woman, a woman who can do it all: the mother to his children, the hot mess in those cutoff jeans, mowing the lawn in her favorite bedazzled baseball cap that reads *#Blessed*. "He who finds a wife," after all, "finds a good thing and obtains favor from the Lord" (Proverbs. 18:22).

How many prospects want all this and a bag of chips? If someone is viewing this from the outside looking in, they would probably holler, "Hell to the no!" Yet, here he is, right now, thinking you're the best thing that ever lived. Instead of rejecting him for the hundredth time, shock him and find your inner string of Christmas lights. Before the kids and the crazy life, there was him. The two of you were the beginning, the reason, the maker of all the goodness. Allow your sexy side to take the lead. Tell the responsible mama that she gets a night off. Allow the lover, the playful girl he met all those years ago on a bus, to step forward. He wants you, girl, in all your raggedy t-shirt glory—he still wants you. And you want him. It's a win-win. You'll be surprised at the return on investment. Set time aside to meet him for lunch. Date him on a random Thursday because the sky is blue. Show the kids that Mom and Dad put each other first.

If money is an issue, have date night in the back-yard. Do something that gives you the time you need to reconnect. You're better together. Hang a *Do Not Disturb* sign on the door. Kids feel most secure when Mom and Dad are strong. No matter how loud they say "Gross!" and roll their eyes, they're watching carefully to mimic your behavior one day. We're teaching them what love looks like in all its facets, from life in the valley, full of heartache and loss, to life on the mountaintop with epic wins. We're teaching them how to fight right and lean in when times are tough.

"Sexy" isn't just the red lipstick and little black dress. "Sexy" is empowered, strong, loud, quiet, and vulnerable. It's lifting one another up in the hard times and celebrat-ing together in the good. It's unconditional when we're thirty pounds heavier than our college days. Would you rather have your partner withhold love because you aren't a certain something, or give you a romantic pat on the butt because he's been with you forever and *loves* you with no expectations or strings attached? I vote Team Unconditional. We choose whether to give love or deny it. Your kids are the fruit of your connection. When we place our spouse as a priority, it's an exponential win.

Are you in a season of life where you have the case of the Don't Want Tos, when you see each other as a bed buddy, when life seems to be in hyper mode? Stop right now. Intimacy and sex are key to a healthy relationship. This is not a safe zone. Stay in this place too long, and the wheels begin to fly off. Pray. God cares about it all. He created you to leave and cleave: "That is why a man leaves his father and mother and is united to his wife, and they become one flesh" (Genesis 2:24). God appreciates that when things are good with your spouse, it's beneficial to the universe.

I have a girlfriend; we'll call her Kelly. When we get together for a night on the town, she always has an interesting story to tell. She said there were days, even weeks when she had nothing to give. She and her husband passed each other like two ships in the night. So, one evening, she prayed and asked God to help her want to want sex with her hubby, to initiate it. To exchange the meek cat mentality for an inner cougar. One night, they're lying in bed and she rolled over, gave him a slight tap on his shoulder, and things accelerated from there. By Friday, their love life had risen to epic status. She couldn't get enough of this man who loved, encouraged, and protected her. Being connected creates intimacy. By Tuesday, he was begging for sleep: "Please, woman, just let me sleep. What's happened to you?" When does a man ever say that? The power of prayer can change everything, ladies. Matthew 7:7 reminds us: "Ask, and it shall be given you; seek, and ye shall find; knock, and it shall be opened until you."

Years ago, when running my video production company, I had a client who was a private investigator. He brought in tapes for me to transfer to DVD for him to use in court cases regarding domestic disputes. It saddened me to view videos of wives and husbands shadily walking into nearby hotels with another person, hand in hand, having an affair on their lunch breaks. I wanted to holler at the tape, "Stop it! You're ruining your life!" in hopes that I could save a marriage. However, it was a video. Those moments had already occurred. Life can become strained as emotions escalate, and chaos ensues. We find ourselves standing on the precipice of life: angry, licking hurt wounds, viewing life from a slanted perspective, comparing *our* enormous duties to *your* lack of them, as we search for a quick escape. Pressures of life become so intense it seems only the cockroaches will survive. Weekly arguments become daily ones. Respect, love, and trust are subtly pushed further down the list. Insecurities generate snarky remarks as go-to's for quick comebacks. That's when the hairline fracture begins, exposing the fault line.

It can start with an innocent business trip or standing in line at a coffee shop. A glance from another person becomes a proposition. Maybe they're a co-worker who dresses to the nines, smells good, and offers the attention you've craved. They don't have bills to pay (or at least not *your* bills). They are free of responsibilities, kids, a barking boss, and a nagging spouse. They're just a good-looking entity, responsibility-free, standing there, thinking you're all fine. Now, as the strength of the chain begins to weaken, you find yourself looking over the fence, thinking if you could walk away from all the pressure, the tangled mess will dissipate. How did you get here? This situation didn't occur overnight. It's been a long time in the making. It's a tiny little weed that placed its first root in the soil and began growing deeper and deeper sight unseen. It's established an entire root system running several feet, creating strongholds lurking beneath. It's a symptom, a manifestation of a deeper problem. If we truly believe our relationship is worth saving, then changing our patterns is a must (either for this relationship or future ones to come). Learn from your mistakes. Outside forces aren't to blame. They're just a face with a name. That guy (or girl, or food, or glass of wine at 10 a.m.) is a mask for pain. If your marriage is stable, a glance in the coffee line or the life that seems easier with the hot guy will go unnoticed.

In the beginning of our marriage, I loved spending money to decorate the house or plan a vacation. Once we had kids, we agreed I could stay home and raise the baby. When we were on one income, money began flying out the window for extra food, activities, baby clothes, a gym membership I seldom used, and tons of lunch dates with friends. John was happy for my new transition but began to frown on my spending habits. I saw it as control. He saw it as planning for our future. I came into this marriage, thinking that if we had checks, we had money. I took a strong stance and didn't budge. The Southern girl in me saw this as a standoff. The engineer in him wanted his crazy wife to be reasonable. After a couple of weeks, he kindly said, "I can't make you stop spending, but if you continue on this path, we will have lots of material things, including overwhelming debt. Would you rather enjoy experiences or acquire another beautiful mirror?" He asked my opinion. He saw me as a partner, and my outlook began to change. My walls of defense began to lower. Because he explained it in a manner that created a partnership, it empowered me to take the reins and decide what our future would look like. Now we're a team. And because we made that decision early on, we created a life plan that allowed us to save money, work from home, and travel with our family. We've lived a life like no other, but we also had to save and sacrifice while building a business and raising four babies born within seven years. It was not easy. I repeat, it was not easy. There were arguments and bad language and meltdowns on the floor (and that was just me). The world tells us marriage should be easy, and that all you need is love. I don't know what they're drinking, but love is only one piece of the puzzle. You need trust, respect, good communication, a plan, and a really good counselor. The whole is greater than the sum of its parts. All those items together create a stronger entity. Respect for one another creates a durable bond. Ranking your partner above the kids, money, and expectations show that you love him for more than what he can provide. Create uninterrupted date nights. Time alone is paramount.

Take an Enneagram or Love Language test to better understand your spouse's personality—how he ticks, how he loves, how he needs to receive love. Create a custom-fit relationship. Authentic love creates a whole host of goodness: "Love is patient, love is kind. It does not envy; it does not boast; it is not proud. It does not dishonor others; it is not self-seeking or easily angered. It keeps no record of wrongs. Love does not delight in evil but rejoices in the truth. It always protects, always trusts, hopes, and always perseveres" (1 Corinthians 13:4-7).

I know what it's like to be with kids all day—dealing with diapers, snacks, and juggling all the things. I know what it's like working in and outside the home as you strive to be all things to all people. I know what it's like to feel overwhelmed and exhausted without an end in sight. Putting your partner first can seem like another task on the list, but he was there before the others came along. Without him, this crazy, amazing life of yours would not exist. Put in the time, the effort, the work to make your marriage healthy and strong.

What if I don't put in the time? What if I don't let the responsible mom take a back seat to the lover at times? Falling in love was easy, but why is staying in love so hard? Girl, you don't *accidentally* own a successful company. You don't *accidentally* have amazing abs and a core. Your kids, with little effort, don't *accidentally* become productive citizens. There are seasons to plant and seasons to reap. Seasons to water and seasons to grow. But if you don't dig, you can't plant. If you don't water, it won't grow. You need tools and resources. If you don't put in the effort, weeds grow, cracks form, and the marriage divides. You may find yourself thirty-six years into a regretful marriage or hiring a PI who gives you a DVD to use as leverage in a divorce case. *What if this relationship is no longer salvageable?* Then take notes and change those tendencies and patterns within yourself.

To think your spouse was 100 percent at fault in all this is defective thinking; it takes two to tango. Don't carry those behaviors to the next stop. A new car, a new relationship, a new city, will not fix what you carry within. The common denominator in all of this is *you*. A marriage is a living, breathing organism. Protect and care for your marriage like the delicate flower that it is. The winds of change can wear it down. Thinking your marriage is exempt from hardship, from an affair, or a divorce is naive. John 10:10 says: "Like a thief in the night, the devil comes to kill, steal and destroy."

Don't you know if he can destroy your marriage, he will try to take it all: the kids, the money, the partnership, the love, a rat-race life filled with unmet expectations and hurt feelings. To think that we don't have to work hard because we already landed our partner is a lie. No one wants to be held hostage by someone that once was. I get it; we all grow older, and gravity sets in, but kindness, love, blessing your other half, and lifting them up will take you to greater heights than you've ever known. A rising tide lifts all boats. Investing in them is investing in you. Your partner is not your slave or your workhorse. They're not just a bed buddy or bill-payer. They are your lover, your best friend.

Be kind, extend grace. Know their love language. Check out Gary Chapman's book *The 5 Love Languages* to better understand if it's receiving gifts, quality time, words of affirmation, acts of service or physical touch. If it's quality time, then take long walks and hang out with one another. Is it touch? Then every time you walk into a room, hold their hand or give them a hug. Buying them roses and chocolates daily isn't financially sustainable, but rubbing their shoulders, feeding them chicken noodle soup on those sick days, being a listening ear when life is overwhelming—this is love. Laughter, tears, babies born, children graduating. This is the ooey-gooey goodness of it all. This is what happens when you put in the effort to make it work. Remember, as a couple, you two came first. Before them, there was him. The rest is a bonus.

Staying in love is work. Life can easily go from a dust storm to a full-fledged hurricane in a heartbeat. We're broken people, carrying emotional baggage from past circumstances. But God uses all things for our good. And whatever *we* do, we should "do it all for the glory of God" (Corinthians 10:31). Nothing is wasted. Bob Goff, author of *Love Does*, reminds us, "It has always seemed to me that broken things, just like broken people, get used more; it's probably because God has more pieces to work with." God isn't asking for perfection, but instead, calls us to show up and do the hard things to create the great ones. For many of us, we go to college, get a job, get married, have 2.5 kids, raise them, become empty nesters, enjoy the grandkids, travel, and the cycle continues into the next generation. (Wow, that's a lot of life in one sentence.) It's all the stuff in the middle that makes staying in love *work*. Love isn't just the kisses and electricity that pulls you together when you first meet. Love goes deeper. Love is a verb. Love *does*.

Love also changes. It looks different as the relationship matures. It's a fight to spend time together. You're swimming upstream, against the rapids, against kid's schedules, against deadlines and distractions. Do what it takes to keep love alive. Need counseling? Get it. Pray for your spouse, pray for your marriage. When life comes at you full force, find each other in the eye of the storm, grab the strand of Christmas lights and hold on. What efforts have you made to show your spouse they are loved and appreciated?

Four Steps to a Solid Marriage

1. List Ways to Show Respect and Love for your partner.

2. How do you best communicate your feelings to your spouse?

3. Describe how you create boundaries for uninterrupted time together.

4. What is your love language, your spouse's love language and how do you show it?

My Prayer

Lord, help me to love my spouse in a way that makes them feel cherished and appreciated. Help me create a marriage that feels safe, secure, and fulfilling. Thank you for giving me a wonderful partner to do life with. I pray you help us to always stay faithful, respectful, and attentive to each other's needs, never taking the other for granted. I pray for an incredible marriage, filled with intimacy and great communication. In Your Name, Amen.

CHAPTER 7
THE VALUE OF A SKINNED KNEE

If you want to be successful, you have to jump.

~Steve Harvey~

A few summers back, we drove a motorhome with four kids cross-country, driving through twenty states in three months, hiking, biking, and paddle boarding through four national parks. It was as crazy as you would imagine, with a husband on constant conference calls, three hungry teens, six pair of stinky shoes, and a little girl with a bossy, I mean, leadership mentality. Winter ski slopes had turned from vast snow-capped mountains to thick grassy knolls, speckled with yellow and white lilies along the foothills. We discovered an extreme mountain bike trail the kids still talk about to this day. As they sat around the bonfire that evening with the fire popping, holding their marshmallow sticks, the words used to describe their ride down the mountain were *epic, exhilarating,* and *death-defying.* They bragged about their skinned-up knees and bloody shins. My son Andrew had a bike crash so horrendous it looked as though he needed a skin graft at best. While their gashes and scratches looked painful, they were delighted to one-up each other on who had the most gruesome scars, as bragging rights for the biggest adventure of the day. Sitting on the sidelines of life was not an option. A skinned knee became their badge of courage.

My daughter, who was too young to bike the trails, felt as though she had missed out on the fun. No one was *ooh*-ing and *ah*-ing over her adventure, so she created one. Undeterred, in her effort to be a part of the conversation, she snuck off—and within minutes, she returned with what looked like a bloody knee. The wife of a retired couple camping to the right of us gasped, "Oh little girl, what happened to your knee?" With tiny pink polished nails and hands clasped over her mouth, she began to giggle, "I drew a bloody kneecap with a red shaw-pee." Our camping neighbors were not amused, as they grabbed their campfire chairs and quickly ran inside, probably thinking we had a mass murderer on our hands.

Often, to keep the knees from getting skinned or an emotional psyche from getting bruised, we sideline our lives from the risks and from the aches and pains it takes to live our dream. We allow fear and past hurts to deny us the aspirations we created in our twenties and the dreams we've held since childhood. Instead, we offer excuses finely crafted to protect us from potential pain.

If you want to do things that have never been done, like being the first in your family to graduate from college, own a business, start a charity, or write a book, then you have to jump out of your current, comfortable life and into the new, challenging one. You can no longer continue to do the same things you've always done, expecting a different result. Comedian Steve Harvey, the author of the book *Jump,* reminds us that every successful person has jumped: "Every person has to take risks. You're either moving forward or backward. You cannot just exist in this life." Ask an entertainer where the jokes originated, and they'll tell you of dark times, struggles, and hard places. The sweetest victories include struggle and conflict, moments of despair, fear, and heartache. Remember that day everything went right? Nope. Rather, our brain records the conflict, the pain of the journey, that brought us to the victories. It remembers the hard work of picking tomatoes on a hot day in June and celebrating with peach ice cream on the front porch swing. Arriving at the top of Mt. Everest by helicopter would feel like cheating. When you bypass the journey, the lesson is lost. We can't fully appreciate the mountaintop until we've walked through the valley. Trials and tribulations create an iron-sharpens-iron effect and climbing out of the trenches develop stamina.

J.K. Rowling's original *Harry Potter* manuscript was rejected twelve times. Thomas Edison spent years inventing a commercially viable light bulb. "I have not failed ten thousand times," he said; "I have not failed once. I have succeeded in proving that those ten thousand ways will not work." Failure is the opportunity to begin again, but next time, a little wiser. Creatives hone their talents to be a better something, a better songwriter, comedian, artist, entrepreneur, software designer, and so on. They are rarely overnight successes. Instead, they are up before dawn, day in and day out, coding on a park bench, trying new recipes while their baby sleeps, or sewing at the kitchen table into the wee hours of the morning. They've designed dozens of products that didn't work or written tons of songs that have never been heard. The world needs what you have to say. They need what you are designing and creating. If you fail, take notes. If you fall, get back up. There's value in a skinned knee. In his "Man in the Arena" speech, Teddy Roosevelt said, "The credit belongs to the man who is actually in the arena, whose face is marked by dust and sweat and blood; who strives valiantly; who errs, who comes short again and again; because there is no effort without error and shortcoming." Those count-less blogs you've written for the masses, read-only by a handful, may have changed lives. Your creation has not gone unnoticed. The falling and getting back up, again and again, has created muscle memory. It's made you stronger and better prepared for the road ahead.

A guy with a gun hollered. "Don't touch it!" These are the words I'll never forget. When visiting a modern art museum, as the kids walked through the exhibits, I noticed a small wooden box the size of a crate sitting in a vast room, encompassed by red velvet ropes, with a vivid spotlight highlighting its treasure. Wow, what was the story behind this exhibit? Was it King Tut's footstool? Why was this rugged wooden box on prominent display? Before I could catch her, my four-year-old ran under the ropes and tried to sit on it. You've never seen such a nimble six-foot-five, three-hundred-pound security guard race across a room so quickly. With embarrassment on our side, we hurriedly grabbed whoever's child this was and set on a journey to find her mother.

My curiosity got the best of me. *What is the backstory on this box?* I wondered. *Why is it being protected with such urgency?* I then read the description. The box had been dragged behind a truck for over a mile to show the wear and tear a rough ride can create. I thought to myself, *Hey kids, look, it's mom on display.* Talk about a conversation piece. My face shows laugh lines that tell stories of good times with friends. It showed the grey hairs on my head that surely came from visiting the Grand Canyon when kids pretended to jump—"Hey mom, whoa, whoa!" I suddenly understood the importance of the rugged box on display. This box, in all its character, represented me. Give this box more security, people. It was obviously more important than King Tut's chair. I saw it as a symbol of my life, raising kids and surviving trials and tribulations. Someone thought it worthy of protection; it quickly became my favorite exhibit, reflecting the realism of what happens when life drags you down. You get knocks and bumps along the way. When we carry a child in our womb for nine months, fly overseas to adopt a child, foster a child, raise our cousin's kid—however we became a mom—life has a way of softening those sharp edges, teaching us to lean in, love harder, and persevere more. The journey is full of trials, tribulations, and skinned-up knees, as well as victories and successes, for this is where true beauty lies. Are you struggling with taking risks and going for your dreams? It's time to live your best life. It's time to step out of your comfort zone and grow wings on the way down.

Are you afraid to fail? Afraid to take risks? Afraid to create? Afraid to downsize your life to create breathing room? Are you afraid to distribute your resume after years of staying home with kids? Have courage. The world is waiting. The world needs what you have to offer. If you don't pursue the dream God has called you to pursue, you're stealing from the world. If you aren't contributing your gifts, He will find someone else who will. Stepping out of your comfort zone is not easy. The perfect circumstances will never arrive. It's time to jump.

What if I fail? What if I look stupid? What if I'm rejected? What other people think about you is none of your business. What do *you* think about you? So, what if it doesn't work out? It may not, at least in the beginning, but you have to jump. Life is full of rejections and what-ifs: Bosses who say no to a promotion, agents who say no to publishing, or kids who say hurtful things that make you want to quit trying. Are you going to accept this rejection as final? No way. This is only an invitation to lean in. This is their no, not your no. Don't allow a simple rejection or hurtful comment to keep you from pursuing your dreams. It's just a code word to press on. Use *no* as a match to ignite the fire.

Rejection and fear are powerful emotions. They can stop you in your tracks, build imaginary barriers, and restrain you from crossing into the land of milk and honey. They can paralyze your dreams, block opportunity, and hold you hostage from the life you've always dreamed. Conversely, they can also spark tenacity and steadfastness. The choice is yours. Press harder, with grit and determination, to be the one who *fails* forward, gets back up, takes notes, and warriors on. What will you choose? Negative people act from their own hurt. Don't allow them to reside in your head, rent-free.

Make sure your worst enemy doesn't live between your ears. - Laird Hamilton

Utilize what God gave you. In life, there's good fear and bad fear. Good fear emerges when the hair on your neck rises to alert you of an intruder (like a black bear that's on your hiking trail) or when that still small voice tells you to run out of a dark alley. Keep this fear in your back pocket. Then there are the what-ifs, the imaginary nothingness of what could happen if we step out to pursue a dream. It's the Great and Powerful Oz behind the curtain—with no real power, just a loud voice. Don't give it space to take root.

What if I don't perform? What if they don't like me? What if I don't get the promotion? What if is the second cousin to *fear*. Working hand in hand as a dynamic duo, they try to stop you from fulfilling your purpose. It's like a date who never showed up or money that never arrived. *If* is commonly used as a conjunction. We can play the *What If* game all day long, but it's a losing battle. *What if* has no answers. A conjunction's purpose is to connect sentences: <u>You will be hungry</u> *if* <u>you don't eat dinner</u>. Without the two independent clauses, you have no purpose, no action, no place to land. *If* is a connector. But without all the nouns and verbs doing the work, the word *if* becomes rogue, like a free-radical causing disease. Left to its own devices, it wreaks havoc and destruction. Let go of the *if*s. They are a dead-end street. Change *if*'s function, and partner it with *I can*: *What if I can write this book with my own perspective and help change the hearts and lives of moms? What if I can help others change their eating habits by creating a healthy lifestyle blog?* See how it changes the dynamics of your situation? Fear, on the other hand, doesn't need a buddy to do its job. It's a stand-alone noun, running around town like the silent bully that it is, distributing empty threats. Fear has the ability to riddle us with terror. It despises words like *risk, contentment, trust, confidence,* and *assurance.* Fear's job is to keep you down in a small box, filled with anxiety, overtaking the next step.

I saw a documentary of an adult elephant that had been chained to a small metal pole since birth. It stood there for years, never understanding the power it had to walk away. Perhaps someone told you, long ago, that you would never amount to anything, that you weren't what they wanted or needed. Time has passed (perhaps the person is long gone), yet you're still tied to the pole of pain. Fear has a way of appearing in the wee hours of the night when no one is around, whispering, "You're going to die, you're going to fail. You don't have the resources. There are hundreds more qualified. You're no expert. You're just another kid who didn't finish high school or get your degree. What could you offer?" We can't allow fear to keep us from truly living.

I changed high schools mid-way through my freshman year. When I was a senior, I decided to get involved in school activities. So, I tried out for cheerleading, band, and school chaplain. I was pure entertainment for those around me. What would Stephanie do *this* week? I tried cheerleading, and the only ones who weren't better than me were small children, senior citizens, and those with leg braces. I ended up as Mascot but opted for a job instead. I ran for Student Chaplain the year prayer was cut from school. I tried out for band, but it was embarrassing driving to the middle school to learn how to play the trumpet with six graders. What if I didn't make it? What if I was rejected? I pushed through all the ifs and jumped like it was my last breath. Though I ended up as neither a cheerleader, a chaplain, or band member, the challenges created strength, they built muscle memory — that I could fall and get back up, and that I could pursue, exert, and go further. It took me out of my comfort zone and created experiences, connections, adventure. Now, I could play a mean "Eye of the Tiger" on my trumpet, do a herkie and say a prayer in front of the masses. (Hey, kids, your mama's got skills.) I knew what I was capable of. Dusting myself off and getting back up taught me that I could do the hard things. Years later, this proved helpful when starting my own business because I wasn't afraid of failure.

Don't be afraid your life will end; be afraid that it will never begin. – Grace Hansen

Remember the story of Joshua in Exodus? After wandering the desert for forty years, the Lord promised the Israelites a land flowing with milk and honey. All they had to do was trust. God fed them on numerous occasions with bread falling from the sky and navigated their way, with miracles at every turn. Yet, when Joshua arrived at the Promised Land, many chose not to enter. Why? They feared what was on the other side, rumors of giants. Some fearfully camped along the wall, on the wrong side of greatness. Don't look back with regret. Let's be the women who walk boldly into the Promised Land, placing our stake in the sand. Like the Israelites who feared, we imagine the worst in life. We turn on the news: the economy is taking a nosedive, terrorism is in our back door, and jobs are being lost at a phenomenal rate. Will our kids go to college? How will we pay the bills? Should we take another job or downsize our home? We form ideas and imagine the worst, and we believe self-fulfilling prophecies that life is not going to be what we thought. We allow fear to dictate where we live and how we move forward.

It's time to rise up and forge ahead. Identify what is holding you back: name it, confront it, and rewrite your story. Rest in the promise that "God will never leave you or forsake you. Do not be afraid; do not be discouraged" (Deuteronomy. 31:8). Grab your mountain bike and head for the hills to live life to its fullest potential. It's time to take the mountain and slay the dragon. Life can leave us rough around the edges. We may come out with a few bumps and bruises, but there's value in a skinned knee. How have you allowed fear to slow you down, and what gave you the courage to warrior on?

Four Questions to Help You Jump

1. What form does your fear take—anxiety, control, perfection? Identify it.

2. What pursuit have you placed on the back burner?

3. What is the worst thing that could happen? What is the best-case scenario?

4. How will you feel in five years if you don't pursue this dream? If you do pursue it?

My Prayer

Lord, thank you for helping me see the difference between the good fear that protects me and the bad fear that keeps me from pursuing my dreams. Help me not to fear failure but to take notes and use them to my benefit. Give me the strength to keep swimming, to keep moving forward, to see those goals come to fruition. Help me to be all that you have called me to be, to fulfill my purpose. In Your Name, Amen.

CHAPTER 8

AMAZING GRACE HOW SWEET THE SOUND

My Grace is made sufficient, and my power is made perfect in weakness.

~2 Corinthians 12:9~

The kids and I were on a twelve-hour road trip to Chicago, driving at 4 a.m. before life had a chance to be disturbed. As the sun rose, so did my crew. In the back seat of our crowded minivan, peaceful sounds of silence turned to sounds of "That's my pillow," "It's cold in here," and "Can we watch a movie?" The gang was up for the day. My husband had been out of town for a couple of weeks. The kids' constant vying for my attention (and sulking loudly in the background when they couldn't get it) began to take its toll. In an instant, I blasted them with the Wrath of Mom, showing my fury like the rage of a dragon, with fire blasting through their little hearts. Immediately, I felt both relief and regret. Surely there was a way to meet in the middle to guide their hearts without burning their ears off with such intensity and frustration. I had to gather my thoughts. As we pulled into a farmer's market on the back end of our journey, my seven-year-old asked if he could go explore. Within a few minutes, he came running back, with glee on his face, excited to see me. (Yes, *excited* to see me—why, when mean mom had just blasted him?) With great pride, he asked me to close my eyes. He handed over a small bag of luxurious dark chocolates, purchased with his chore money. "You're the best mom ever," he said, "and I appreciate all the things you do for us to make life happy and good." Cue the puddle on the floor.

I was given unconditional love that day. Tears may have bypassed my tear duct and shot straight out of my eyeball. My son had worked hard all week on his chores, washing laundry and vacuuming, and with his spoils bought me a prize. I didn't deserve it, but he saw the goodness in my efforts and wanted to bless me with grace in the form of chocolates.

But what happens when someone doesn't extend you grace for something that was just an accident or a mistake? It's like placing salt on a wound. If someone breaks your favorite lamp, it's easy to scream and yell, but it was a mishap, not malice. No one wants to disappoint, and yet there we are hollering and scolding. What if, instead of yelling, we extended favor? What if we lift their spirit instead of pouncing on their soul? Like a fork in the road, choosing exasperation or gratitude will change the course of a relationship. That day, there was a paradigm shift in our connection, and when I asked for forgiveness after my son extended grace, our bond became stronger. "See to it," says Hebrews 12:15, "that no one falls short of the grace of God and that no bitter root grows up to cause trouble and defile many." Kyle Idleman, author of *Grace is Greater*, expounds on this:

> *When we miss grace, a bitter root begins to grow. In the Hebrew culture, any poisonous plant could be called a "bitter" plant. The author of Hebrews uses bitter root as a metaphor to make it clear that when we miss grace, things become toxic. Religion without grace is poisonous. A relationship without grace is harmful.*

God wanted us to experience what only He could give by offering three types of grace. First, there's saving grace: the gift of salvation, not earned, but only received through redemption from the cross. Confessing that Jesus is Lord and believing that He died on the cross for your sins brings salvation. Next is sanctifying grace: the world is quick to judge and the first to condemn, drawing attention to all your faults and sinful ways, but God gently convicts from within, bringing personal change minus the criticism. Last is serving grace: the power to minister and bless others through ministry, missions, or the giving of our time, gifts, and resources. We all experience growth, change, and transitions; we are always becoming. God saw this and gave us saving grace when we were born again. Like newborn infants, starting over, He bought us with a price. Then as we grew, He offered sanctified grace, knowing that as spiritual toddlers and teenagers, we would need grace for growth to free us from sin, creating personal conviction deep in our soul. As we matured, we give back to others what has been given to us through serving and ministry. God offered us grace, and the least we could do is pay it forward. What an awesome example of amazing grace.

Do you struggle with grace? Do you labor over why you don't deserve it? Do you over-analyze your analyzation? With a choice of extending grace or yelling negatives, which is quicker on the tongue? For me, by far, the negative is easier. Positive talk needs more brainpower. Want to train your brain to be more positive? Surround yourself with more positive people. Gravitate toward those who lift you up. Encourage someone else. Give a shout-out to inspire another. Give them your parking spot or pay for their coffee. In a world of negativity, your actions will shine like a beacon in the night. It will change another's perspective and lighten their load. Grace is free for the taking. It's like an unexpected present under the tree with your name on it—in June. It's yours with no strings attached. Whether you receive it—or opt-out instead—will determine your story. We can read in Ephesians 2:8, "For it's by grace you have been saved, through faith, and this is not from yourselves, it is a gift of God, not by works, so that no one can boast." How appropriate that our own children demonstrate God's kindness, mercy, and grace when we didn't do a thing to earn the favor, yet here we are on the receiving end. It's given me a whole new understanding of how His mercy is new every morning. When we place ourselves on an earn-to-love program, we fall short most days. God is our Father, and grace is given just because you are His. In the precious position you hold as a mom, you are needed and loved by your children, even on the bad days. And just about the time you believe the lie that you're not a good parent, remember, of all the people in the world, you are the only one your kids need and want most. So, how lucky are you?

What if we don't extend ourselves grace and keep listening to the doubt? You'll go down in a blaze of glory and take everything you deemed important down with you. You're the hub of communication, the captain of the ship. Your attitude and perspective set the tone for your family. If you're always frustrated, always speaking negative thoughts, then your children will step in behind you and mimic your actions. You hold more power than you think. Clean up your act, sister, and give yourself permission to be human. It's okay to mess up and ask for forgiveness, to not have the cleanest house on the block; you don't need to hustle for your worth.

As you spend your days loving, teaching, protecting, it seldom feels like enough. You're behind at every turn, drowning in the to-do list that continues to grow. The kids need a quick school lunch, and all you've got is a frozen chimichanga while the neighbor's mom sent homemade chicken noodle soup. You don't know their story, and they don't know yours. Last week, she may have forgotten to pick her son up at soccer practice, and he ate dinner with the coach's family. I guarantee you *that* story won't end up on social media as a brag for the week.

You tell yourself, *my children would have better opportunities if a more organized and time-management-savvy mama raised them.* So, you punish and question yourself, heaping guilt on like the good shoveler you are. You believe you are not the right fit for your kids because sometimes you holler, sometimes you're late for school, and sometimes you feed them snacks with Yellow Dye #5 for dinner. You're sure this further substantiates that you're an incapable, crappy mom. So, you begin to hustle for your worth. You begin to volunteer more, clean faster, run harder. You say yes more, determined to prove your value, to justify your place on the family tree.

Remember, the God who created the heavens and the earth, who made the moon and the stars, and did it all in seven days, created you to be their mama. No *if*s, *and*s, or *but*s. You're it. You fit like peanut and jelly, like two peas in a pod. There's no opportunity to earn your spot—because, through grace, it's yours. You can't earn the calling. You *are* the calling. So, quit trying to prove God wrong. You were made for this position, whether you're a single mom, a stepmom, a bonus mom, or an aunt raising her sister's kids. Those blessings were placed in your hands to be raised, loved, and cared for by you. So, no more second-guessing your spot. This is your moment, girl. Now go forth in your Cheerio-filled minivan and take your place like a motha!

I organized a Mom's Night Out event. We put together amazing speakers, with a desire to encourage and feed into the souls of all the mamas. The attendees were a mix of stay-at-home moms and career moms, ranging from moms of preschoolers to empty nesters. We asked them to anonymously write on a sticky note the self-doubts they told themselves on a regular basis. Here's what was written:

> *I can't accomplish my dreams and raise kids simultaneously.*
> *I'm a bad mom.*
> *I'm fat. How can anyone love me?*
> *I'm too much for people.*
> *I'm not beautiful enough, not smart enough.*
> *It's my fault my kids failed at something.*
> *I can't do anything right.*
> *I'm messing up my children.*
> *I should be further along.*
> *I'm too old to make a difference.*
> *I'm not worthy.*
> *I'm too old to start a new career.*
> *I don't have a clue what I'm doing.*
> *I will never be a good enough wife.*

But the note that repeated itself the most—drum, roll please—was: *I'm not enough.* It was written on sticky notes over and over again: in every type of handwriting, on every color of sticky note, by every type of mom, in every stage of life. Scattered throughout the wall, *I'm not enough.* Not enough what? The self-doubt was too vague to fight. Too obscure to nail down. Can you identify with any of these voices of self-doubt?

Upworthy.com produced a video asking kids to describe their moms. Here's their perspective:

> *She's funny.*
> *My mom cooks for me.*
> *She cuddles with me.*
> *She gives the best hugs after school.*
> *We go to church together.*
> *She's my heart.*
> *My mom is my hero.*

Hmmm, apparently, they view us moms through rose-colored glasses. Maybe we should buy a pair. At times, we're a mess and a masterpiece, but most of all, we're enough.

The self-doubt I hear originates from a familiar place. No one has ever approached me at Target and told me I sucked at being a mom. No one has ever walked up to me on the street and expressed that I'm not enough. That I should be further along. That I'm a terrible cook. Let me tell you who the culprit is. If I listen hard enough, the girl telling me these lies has a Southern accent. It's weird—she sounds just like me, telling me I'm not enough, telling me my butt is too big, telling me that I'm too old or too late to make a difference. That I could be doing more. The message comes in the form of judgment, as we compare ourselves to others: like the time, I saw a corporate mom dropping off her kids at school dressed in a suit. I compared my ratty ponytail to her styled hairdo.

The message came again when I misread what I thought was rejection from a friend who didn't call back when she had a family emergency. Oh, the self-doubt I've created.

My oldest son told his little brother that he couldn't play with him because of Algebra homework. The little one came running in with disappointment in his voice, "Mom, he doesn't want to play with me." I asked, "Is that *really* what he said?" We are receiving signals from a biased TV antenna. Did we *really* hear what was said, or did we translate the message through our own feelings of insignificance and lacking? Ladies, it's time to get maintenance on the antenna. Change the tune you hear to "Amazing Grace How Sweet the Sound."

We were placed in this position for such a time: to love, create, teach, raise, discipline, and shepherd hearts. We were placed on this earth to dream big, to walk in our purpose, and write our story. Life ebbs and flows. Some days we're on our game, and other days we need a little grace. We don't need six-pack abs, an MBA or a cooking show to prove our position, to prove we belong, to prove we are a good-enough something. Kids are going to mess up. But we don't get rid of them. Instead, we lean in and love harder. And if you look around, no one cares if you can't cook a fancy dinner. They just want a mean mac and cheese. We won't always have our college body. We won't always be twenty-three or thirty-five, but we have life experiences under our belt. It's never too late to start a new career or a new chapter as long as you have breath and are willing. People need what you have to offer. Let go of the self-doubt. Let go of other people's expectations of what they want or need you to be and write your story. I am a good mom. I'm the best one they've got. We all make mistakes.

Life isn't perfect. But we dust ourselves off and forge ahead. Like a GPS, when we get off course, life re-calculates. Our actions, our behaviors, don't always merit favor, but God gives us grace because we are His. So, when the road trip of life calls on you at 4 a.m. with situations hurled at top speed . . . step back, grab a piece of chocolate, and remember: "Because of God's great love, we are not consumed. His grace, His mercies are new every morning. Great is His faithfulness" (Lamentations 2:22-23).

Four Questions to Finding Grace

1. How could you speak words of life to encourage others?

2. In weeding out any bitterness, what would you remove first?

3. In what areas could you give or receive more grace?

4. What does grace look like to you?

My Prayer

Lord, help me to truly understand that I've always been enough because I'm your child, redeemed by Your cross. Thank you for gently convicting me, without judgment, to be the best person I can be, to bless and serve others. Help me to live to my full potential for your glory. In Your Name, Amen.

TRANSITION 3:

BECOMING

CHAPTER 9

SAVOR THE MOMENTS

Life moves pretty fast. If you don't stop & look around once in a while, you could miss it.

~Ferriss Bueller~

Can anyone remember what life was like before kids? Anyone? I know I surely took it all for granted: sleep, extra money, a chicken-nugget-free car, travel on a whim, smudge-free windows, cute outfits that smelled like Downey. It's hard to believe that used to be me. While sitting in traffic, I noticed a man in an orange Lotus sports car with stick figure decals on the back window. Instead of decals with the typical mom and dad and all their kids, this guy had a decal of him and his wife holding bags of money. I wasn't sure whether to ram his car or give him a fist bump for being smarter than the rest of us. Reeling from the Lotus guy, I passed a minivan with a bumper sticker that read, *I used to be cool*. I totally get this woman. I want to have coffee and share war stories with her.

Continuing on, I pulled into Target, herding four kids under the age of seven. As we entered the toy department, my five-year-old decided he wanted to touch everything he saw on Aisle Seven. Because of his success, his little brother thought it would be cool to push everything he saw on Aisle Six. Items were flying off shelves faster than I could give them the Mom Look. (I love this superpower.) In an effort to ease tension, I delegated pushing the cart with the baby inside to my oldest child. I grabbed two little boys' hands and gently guided them down the middle aisle, quietly threatening their lives if they touched one more item. In the corner of my eye, I observed an elderly woman slowly walking towards me. What did she want? Why was she smiling? She waltzed up and said, "These are the best days of your life."

"I don't know about that," I quickly retorted.

"Yes, these are the best days." And just like that, she was gone. I didn't have to time to wrestle her to the ground and say, "Take it back, lady." If these were *the best days*, why didn't she help me with one of the four? Maybe change a diaper or feed a kid while I measured the seven-year-old for his shoe size.

Now let me pause because my first thought was *not* Pretty! An attitude of crazy wanted to rise to the top. As I slowly regained my eyesight and my upper lip stopped twitching, I envisioned a guy hanging off the side of a helicopter swirling through the sky, holding a bull horn, yelling: "Stephanie, don't jump!" If this is *the best*, then we've got a problem. Something is 'bout to go down. I was hoping for, "Hang in there. It gets better." Lie to me.

If someone dangles a carrot of hope, I can keep going, but telling me this is *it*—We have arrived at the station! These are *the best days!*—left me exiting the store like a deflated balloon. I could have walked across the street, never seeing oncoming traffic, thinking this *is it*? I've heard horror stories of rebellious teenagers. Heck, I was one myself. But hearing, "These are *the best days*," left me in a state of despair.

As I lay in bed in the dark hours of the night pondering what she meant, I began to assess my life, our situation: the crazy, loud life of raising a swarm of kids so close in age. I couldn't help but laugh at the memory of my six-year-old still wearing his red, dinosaur-spiked bike helmet while practicing his violin. Or my four-year-old writing the words *left* and *right* on the top of his new tennis shoes with a Sharpie so he wouldn't forget. If we are willing to redefine what is good in our lives, then these are *the best days*. If we could see our life for what it is—not the unrealistic expectations of what it could be—and if we understand that our house is going to look like seven squirrels live in it, then our mindset will change. Instead of taking things too seriously and always seeing the negative aspects, we should lighten up and think about what we would do if the kids weren't here. Okay, a trip to Italy comes to mind, but for the long haul, this journey we're on—leading, guiding, loving—this adventure eventually leads to them leaving the nest. Embrace the good, the messy, and the loud. The next time you are walking the aisles, gaining attention from judgmental eyes, smile, and whisper to yourself, "These are *the best days* because they are mine!"

When I was a kid, my fondest memories were the days my little sister and I jumped off our boathouse into the lake, giggling as we ran toward the house eating peach ice cream and dodging sprinklers on our way to the trampoline. We had so much fun, but I'm not sure when it stopped. If only I had known, that was our last day, swimming and singing our favorite songs, recorded on my red 1982 tape recorder. Y'all, she was the cutest little being with blonde pigtails. She was my real-life baby doll. We stood up for one another, and we were partners in crime. It was just the two of us, and that was all we needed. And then, one day it all stopped. Perhaps our attention turned to other things. Summer ended. We moved on. I'm not sure. But if I had known it would be our last carefree summer, surely, I would have embraced it harder, enjoyed it more.

Time waits for no one. Now my oldest is headed to college. When he was small, he loved being thrown in the air. It made him laugh uncontrollably. I think he lost weight giggling! I look back on those fond memories with laughter and sadness because I had no idea that throw #399 would be the last toss, the last giggle. A new phase came along, and just like that, it was over. Time doesn't stop for our reflection. Life doesn't throw up a red caution flag to warn us, *This child won't think you're fun or smart in seventeen days.*

My three-year-old used to scream "A bridge!" every time we crossed one. I had anxiety each time I saw a bridge, knowing he would randomly shout "A bwidge!" all day long as our minivan navigated through town. And then one day, as I braced myself for a drive over the canal, he didn't say a word. In fact, he never said, "A bwidge!" ever again. That morning was the last time, and I felt sad, realizing the toddler years had closed that day, and I wasn't ready.

From the moment they leave the womb, our children are leaving us. Every day, minute by minute, they are growing up and gradually moving farther away. Make the moments count! Savor them. Did you realize when you gave your child a piggyback ride when he was seven that it would be the last time? I had no idea. Now he's in middle school, and time is slipping away. No one told me it was the last time I would ever hold him. Now I'm on the floor, kicking and screaming. I was robbed. I guess I could pick him up now. Of course, I might get a hernia, and he'll think I'm crazy, but we'll both remember when I picked him up last! Embrace all the moments. This could be family vacation #101 of #102. We just don't know. This could be the last one-on-one conversation about their childhood, laughing and crying over a life well lived under your roof, as they leave for college. Life is short, so savor the moments.

They say you can't see the forest for the trees. In order to gain a new perspective on the goodness I had in my life, I needed to savor the moments. I had to step away, collect my thoughts, and re-strategize. It's easy to establish a negative pattern as we get stuck in the same old routines. That's when we tend to step into busyness and hurriedness, which can distract us from savoring the goodness. Want ideas for gaining a new perspective? Here's what worked for me. I called my kids and listened to their voices on the phone. They sounded so much younger and more innocent than I remembered. Instead of negotiating and wrangling with the teens on how they feel, sometimes the best conversations would unveil themselves on a long walk, an evening by the fire pit, or conversations on the back-porch swing. Believe me, making time for connection works. The urge to meltdown over the slightest mishaps will fade away. Patience, understanding, and communication make way for a stronger connection.

Secondly, when life comes at you, full speed ahead, it's important to be your own gatekeeper. Establish boundaries and parameters. Overbooked schedules tend to bring out our worst behavior. And those closest to us are often affected most. What affects you affects the family. Protect the nest. You're the boss. Your kids look to you as their guide. Establishing boundaries creates stability and security for them (and for you!).

And lastly, cultivate an atmosphere that suits your family. For example, what dreams and goals do you want to accomplish together? Are you a family that loves to travel, or that has a fondness for history, reading, sports, hiking, or photography? Cultivate this atmosphere. In doing so, you'll create a tie that binds. For us, we love to go motorhome camping, mountain biking, and hiking the national parks. As a family, it's created incredible bonding time, fire pit moments, and connections that we'll share for years to come. Sit down with your family, discuss what type of atmosphere best fits you, and cultivate it.

The days are long, and the years are short. Life's clock is on a countdown. Our kids are growing up so fast. We're rushing to sports activities, and meaningful conversations are left unsaid. You skid into carpool, and the last words spoken were, "I don't have the time."

Do you want to be the lyrics to Harry Chapin's song, "Cats in the Cradle?" He reminds us that if we're too busy, one day, our kids will follow in our footsteps, and they'll choose work and other interests over spending time with us. We are teaching them that time with family is ranked midway down our priority list. We're allowing distractions, technology, deadlines, and futile obligations to detour our *why*—the reason for it all. Embrace all the moments with your kids, big and small. One day, you will get to pee in peace and eat the last cookie in broad daylight without sharing. People say, "Hold on to every moment because they grow up so fast." It's true. One minute your kids are dragging around their favorite blankie, and the next, they're driving away in the car.

One morning I woke up, and amongst all the chaos of daily activity, my six-month-old baby was in Second Grade and politely asking me not to kiss him at the bus stop. My teenagers are so busy with sports, homework, and friends that I have to schedule myself into their calendar. Just yesterday, I was their entire world, and today, I'm only a piece of it. Finding time together is challenging. We often focus on the task at hand, frustrated by how our kids need us for everything—without realizing that in seven days, they won't ask anymore. One minute, they'll tell you a three-minute story that takes seventeen minutes, making you want to lose your mind, but the next, you won't be the one they make a beeline to. Don't be too quick to shoo them away. They won't always fight for a hug or give you a million kisses.

It's vital to soak up all the moments, good or bad, whether it's singing in the car or crying on the floor. They are your moments. You'll look back and wish you had those times again. Of course, you won't miss the screaming in the back seat or the arguments you have with your teen, but you'll miss *them*. You can't edit out the negatives. It's all or nothing, the whole package. I know it sounds ridiculous, but you will miss it. When you have to load up the baby and take him to carpool with the older kids, it can feel exasperating, but believe me, you'll miss it. This is your future speaking. I've been on both sides of the fence, and you *will*.

What if I can't see the good in difficult situations? You don't understand, my house is a wreck and my day never ends. How can I believe these are good days if my life is full of rebellious teenagers, poopy diapers, and a kitchen that's always a mess? What if the chaos outweighs the goodness? Well, then you'll miss the true meaning of it all. While the toddler is puking, he looks up and sees the first person to arrive on the scene with love and compassion: his mama. You're building strong connections. When your teen comes home from school, lashing out at you, from being bullied and downtrodden as the world cruelly hits them at every turn, who is right there with a shoulder to lean on?

You're creating unbreakable bonds. When you can't see the speck of goodness in a forest of calamity, climb higher. Do what it takes to grab a bird's-eye view. You are forming robust relationships for a lifetime. Don't be so focused on the doing, the feeding, the technical parts, that you miss the ooey-gooey goodness of the journey. Ecclesiastes 1:2 says, "Life is fleeting, like a passing mist. It's like trying to catch hold of a breath. It all vanishes like a vapor." And it's so very true. So, bend down and hug them. Squeeze that soft little leg and high-five the littles. Insert yourself into the teen's busy schedule. My five-year-old reminds me, "Mom, you're the best mom I've ever had." It's true: I'm the one and only. And you're the only one who has the God-given privilege to do this job, so make it count. There are days when you want it to fly by. It's pure labor with the littles and critical thinking prowess with the teens. Each level has its own difficulties. Savor the moments, for this too shall pass.

Follow Solomon's advice from Ecclesiastes 9:7, "Eat bread with gusto, drink wine with a joyful heart. God takes pleasure in your pleasure. Relish life with those you love, each and every day of your precarious life, for every day is a gift." Ask God for guidance. He is the answer, your North Star. When God assigns you such a Great Commission, He promises to be with you always, to the end of the age. He will lead you, guide you, bless and protect you. Jesus says in John 15:5, "Apart from Me, you can do nothing." God knows how you feel. Lay the truth on the table. Pray for wisdom on how to proceed. Your emotions won't derail God.

Do you feel despair, rage, agitation or shame? You can't throw a curveball that the good Lord hasn't seen. In our weakness, He is strong. The devil wants us to fail, scream, to fight with our kids and even our spouse, with chaos at every turn. Stay the course, mama. Focus on what really matters. Life is not perfect. There are days you want to give up. The laundry, the dishes, the kids fighting, the complaints about what you made for dinner—it can all be overwhelming. Take a deep breath and listen to a song that makes you feel empowered. Scream and dance in the closet. Do whatever you need to press on and fight harder. Laugh at the craziness. Remember those nights you prayed for them before they were born. This is your moment to shine. So, say it: "These are *the best days,* for they are mine."

Shauna Niequist, author of *Present over Perfect,* reminds us of the lie we tell ourselves: "If you do more, you are more. Life is too fast, too full and too busy. It's important to live life to the full and not live life to the busy." I couldn't agree more. Busyness does not equal importance. I repeat —busyness does not equal importance. We go, go, go until the wheels fly off, 'til we're exhausted to the point of no return. Do you cover up your pain by upgrading the kitchen, buying a new car, or adding another gold star to your resume? We rarely change our patterns until our threshold is maxed out and we hit rock bottom. We run ourselves ragged until we hit the wall.

Perhaps you're in the middle of a divorce, fighting with a friend, dealing with health issues, pondering the point of it all. Maybe you're trying to start a business or sell a business and you've missed important events. You're too exhausted to lift another finger, contemplating, *How did I get here?* It's time to do the work, head to the trenches, dig up the root, and start again. It's time for a do-over or a makeover. You may feel like your life has burned to the ground, but hold on, girl. Dust yourself off and start again. It's time for a reset to scrub down the to-do list, to learn to say no, and to focus on what's important. We need time together to create connections, to establish a legacy. If you're lucky, you have eighteen summers with your children. That's it. Eighteen under one roof. It's time to invest in s'more moments, game nights, and after-dinner walks. "For what is your life, but a mist that appears for a time and then vanishes" (James 4:14)? God paired you with your family to create meaningful moments, to slow down and savor each because it could be the last time. When you're hauling littles or guiding teen hearts, what activities can you establish to assure busyness never overrides the goodness of the journey? How will you use the time to assure that right here, right now, these moments are *the best days,* for they are mine?

Four Steps to Savoring the Moments

1. List two ways you can savor life's little moments.

2. How do you step away from the chaos to hear your inner voice?

3. What does it look like when you re-connect with yourself? How does it feel?

4. Find space in your calendar to hear your voice, God's voice. What does this look like?

My Prayer

Lord, help me to create slow-down moments to savor the journey. It's so easy to live in a hurried state, but in doing so, I could miss out on *the best days*. Show me ways to carve out breathing room, to seize life, and enjoy the ooey-gooey goodness of the journey. In Your Name, Amen.

CHAPTER 10

STEERING A CATEGORY 5 HURRICANE

Come to me all who labor and are heavy laden
and I will give you rest.

~Matthew 11:28~

Do you remember when you were little, swinging at the park so high that your toes touched the sky? You squeezed those metal chains as you flew through the air. When it was time to let go, your hands hurt from the grip. What did it feel like, holding on so tightly? We had an uncle pass away, the first to go of seven siblings. Talk about the life of the party; Uncle Jerry knew how to celebrate. That day, we would celebrate him in the form of a balloon release at a roadside funeral service. We drove through two states to lay him to rest in a small town with a population of 8,756. It brought back so many memories: from the old Dairy Delight to the new Walmart, everyone fought to keep out (to assure mom-and-pop stores continued to thrive). It had such a down-home feel. The community was brought together with Friday Night Lights, fishing on the weekend, and the old used car dealership on Main Street. Aside from the First Baptist Church, the most popular gathering spot was the Winn Dixie. It was the Who's Who of hangouts in a town full of local businesses like Bobby Joe's Car Wash and Tim's Garage.

After driving for hours, we met my parents at a local drug store to pick up fifty helium balloons for a balloon release that day. Walking through the drug store, the kids grabbed funny objects that only a small town could offer: like beer can chimes and "All you need is Jesus and the SEC" coffee mugs. There were laughs and "Hey Mom, look at this" for half an hour. My oldest son had been eating chocolate while we loaded balloons. "Buddy, go to the bathroom and clean your face," I instructed. My husband wrestled the fifty blue helium balloons into the car, as gusts of wind blew them out the other side. My Uncle Bobby, Jerry's brother, laughingly videotaped us sparring with the gazillion balloons that continued to creep their way into the driver's seat. At this point, the entire car was filled with balloons that had a mind of their own. Humans would need to find another ride. About the time that twelve balloons were secure, four more shot out the front window. The kids were laughing as they slammed balloons back into the car. Ten minutes later, our caravan was on its way. We sent the kids with my parents, who were feeding them a steady stream of chocolate bars. Best day ever.

Upon our arrival at the roadside service, I observed the most beautiful ten acres of lush green grass, overflowing kudzu, and colorful flowers. It seemed as though everyone in town was represented. Cars were parked along the road for what felt like miles. As soon as we opened the car door, the wind gave our hair follicles a run for their money. The hour of fixing hair with the precise amount of Aqua Net, wasted. Balloons slammed to the ground, *Boom, Ba, Boom, Boom.* Three hit the ground and popped. As I wrestled balloons and a hairdo that once was, my cell phone rang.

"Uh, hey, Mom, where are you?"

Boom, Boom. There went two more.

"Who is this?" I asked.

The wind was howling so loud, I could barely hear a voice on the other line.

"It's your son."

"Who?"

"Your son, Jack. Where are you, Mom? You left me at the drug store."

"What? I thought you were riding with Grandpa."

I had written down the plan, but now I'd left a child in a town he'd never visited, in a state he didn't live in, stranded at a drug store he'd never been to. And just as I'm trying to figure out who to blame. *Boom,* there goes another balloon.

"You told me to go to the bathroom and wash my face. When I came out, everyone had left."

Boom!

"Listen, buddy, mama is responsible for a balloon release. This is of utmost importance, and I can't pick you up".

"Uh, ok."

Bang. Bang. Hair is flying, and balloons are slamming to the ground. I'm down to thirty-five.

Oh, dear God.

"Ok, here's the plan. Your Uncle Bobby will drive over and pick you up."

"Who?"

"Now, I know you don't remember him. He's wearing a black trench coat and a black hat. Get in the car with him."

Silence . . .

Everything this child ever learned about stranger danger, I'd thrown out the window.

"Uh, are you sure?" he asked.

"Yes. He'll walk into the drug store. So be looking for him and his black trench coat. The password is . . . Uncle Bobby."

Poor child. Throw another dollar into the Counseling Bucket. He's gonna need it.

Bam. Thirty-four!

As Van Morrison's song says, "There'll be Days Like This." No matter how much you plan, fix, and prepare, life is not in your control, no matter how tight the grip. It's like trying to wrestle a Category Five hurricane and steer it in a different direction. It's false security. I didn't want to place the outcome in another's hands. I may have had a few superpowers, but control wasn't one of them. Control is rooted in fear, and fear cultivates worry, anxiety, and trepidation. I needed to let go to spur trust, flexibility, and freedom.

But I had to figure out how to let go. I had to find a way to free myself from the emotional torture of believing I had the power to sway life's outcome: so, I began to pray. I began to place my worries at the foot of the cross. "Do not fear, for I am with you, do not be dismayed, for I am your God. I will strengthen you and help you; I will uphold you with my righteous right hand" (Isaiah 41:10). I didn't have to go it alone. When problems beyond my control occurred, what I could control was my reaction and behavior.

Are you rigid in your plans? Do words like *flexibility* and *Plan B* make you cringe? If your arrangements fail or life doesn't go your way, do others suffer? Why do you hold on so tightly? We fear the unknown. We fear negative outcomes. Rick Warren, the pastor of Saddleback Church, wrote an article titled "Let Go and Know God is In Control." In it, he says, "Whenever we face out of control situations, we tend to go to one of two extremes. For some of you, the more out of control life gets, the harder you try to control it. Or you do the opposite: You just give up. You have a pity party and invite yourself to it." I've been on both sides of this battle, and I'm here to tell you, you won't win. Life is not perfect; rather, it's a journey of progress. We are fallible humans, not angels or God. We're just people who live in a sinful world with an iniquitous nature, trying to make our way in an unpredictable world.

Do you think that, by holding on so tightly, you'll find order or keep the kids from getting hurt? Do you think by bundling them in bubble wrap, they won't fall? Do you think that, by loving them more than others, they won't succumb to illness? Do you think that, by clamping on tighter, you'll keep bad things from happening? You may think, *But Stephanie, you don't understand. If I don't steer my kids to the right college, they won't find the perfect spouse, and their life path will be ruined. What if they miss out on a career opportunity?*

Oh, the pressure. Dear Mama, put your fake magical powers back into the magician's kit and take a breath. This is not your burden to bear. However, you can pray, trust God, and ask for support from other moms going through similar situations. This is not your wheel to steer. You may think you have to keep complete control or something bad will happen. I assure you that if you don't let go, it will. *But if I don't hold tightly, who will?* Do you think an innocent child who dies of cancer is loved by their parents any less? No matter how tightly you hold, how hard you love, life happens. It's not in our hands. Let it go. At the end of Uncle Jerry's funeral, his precious wife walked over and took the remaining helium balloons, with only nine left. As they whipped in the wind, she closed her eyes, whispered to her beloved and gently released them. She wasn't responsible for where they blew, how far, or how high, but they would never have made it to their destination if she hadn't done her part and let go.

> *That is why I tell you not to worry about everyday life—whether you have enough food and drink, or enough clothes to wear. Isn't life more than food, and your body more than clothing? Look at the birds. They don't plant or harvest or store food in barns, for your heavenly Father feeds them. And aren't you far more valuable to Him than they are? Can all your worries add a single moment to your life?* Matthew 6:25-26

You can send your kids off to school, and they can be bullied, get dropped from a team, or make a bad grade. You could burn calories trying to control the uncontrollable, listing all the terrible things that could happen. You turn on the news and see war, death, and poverty all around. A drunk driver kills a family on the same section of interstate you had driven through moments earlier. You can choose to live in turmoil, biting your nails, losing your hair, and fearing the sky will fall—or you can live in the present and count life precious. You can pray, trust and believe that no matter what happens, God is in control. You have a choice: to listen to the giggles in the living room as the kids tell stories and rehash their day or be too busy to see the goodness in front of you. Let go of the hurt. Let go of the future. Let go of the past. Let go. "You can never move forward if you're always looking back," writes Susan Miller, author of *After the Boxes are Unpacked.*

What if I let go? Am I telling the world that I don't care that I don't love them? That couldn't be further from the truth. *What if I forgive? Will it look as though I've conceded? Am I letting them off the hook? If I forgive, does it mean I allow them back in my life?* Not at all. But in the letting go, in the forgiveness, you are freeing yourself of anger and resentment. It's not about them; it's about you. If you don't let go, if you don't forgive, it's as though you are drinking poison and hoping it harms the other person. A friend wronged you, a parent disowned you, or a relationship treated you badly, and you keep thinking it's salvageable. You may have had an alcoholic father who made you feel like you were never enough, an emotionally abusive mother who perpetuated the behavior, a friend who misunderstood, or a neighbor who quit talking to you one day. Perhaps you wrote letters and texted, trying to discuss, to make amends, to repair the damage and apologize for a mess you may or may not have helped create, but all to no avail. The entire situation is a jumbled mess, but they're not willing to work it out. Some people walk away. You may think, "if only they would reply." But no reply *IS* a reply. Some are unwilling or are no longer on this earth as you wrestle with emotions that feel tangible.

You've rehearsed this conversation in your head a million different ways, trying to make sense of it all. You have told them off, stated your claim, and made your case, and yet you still feel angry and are left reeling inside. Your lens of life is skewed through how they made you feel. Your story and life patterns have you seeking perfection, hustling for approval, struggling to be enough, holding control as if you were appointed to save it all. Guess what? Life's circumstances are out of your control. But you still spend days, weeks, and even years trying to obtain it. You want to tell the world what happened and how you were wronged, but it doesn't matter. You can only control your reactions, your thoughts, and your emotions. To think you are 100 percent fault-free would be a delusion. Some relationships will never be resolved, and you have to let go. For the sake of your health, your family, your sanity. Let it go.

What will happen if I relinquish control? In letting go, it will feel as though the weight of the world has lifted. It's no longer your job to be the gatekeeper of others, but rather the boundary-line drawer of yourself. How you choose to move forward—whether as a victim or as victorious—is up to you. Moses wandered the desert for forty years with a caravan of six hundred thousand freed Israelites and their families. He was responsible for leading them to the Promised Land. He wanted all the answers every step of the way. He asked, "God, how are we going to cross the Red Sea?" So, God parted it.

"How are we going to feed such a large crowd?" God rained down bread from heaven, producing miracles for 40 years and yet Moses continued to struggle with trust and control. God, how will you provide water? Moses wanted to know and know now. He was mad at the impatience he faced from thousands of slaves, and yet he was acting similarly. God told Moses to smite the rock, and water would flow, quenching their thirst in the desert. But Moses, in his anger, acted as if the water was provided by him and not God and struck the rock twice. For this, Moses wasn't allowed to enter the Promised Land. Ouch. How frustrating to miss the boat, to miss the goodness, to miss the fruit of your labor. He walked in the desert for forty years and missed the finale due to control issues.

Do you remember those holiday Coca Cola ads with the Norman Rockwell paintings? Rockwell perfectly captured the essence of what Christmas could be. There was no Drunk Uncle Ed in his paintings. No one had to deal with klepto Aunt Claudia. There was no fighting at the kitchen table over who ate the last piece of fried chicken. Rockwell's paintings were the essence of perfection in American culture. We, on the other hand, were not. Our family was more like a National Lampoon Christmas Vacation, with kids flying down the stairwell in a snow sled, knocking out spindles, while fighting over who had to wash the dishes. My dad told me once that I had a Norman Rockwell mentality, and if I didn't repair this mindset, I would have a difficult path ahead. Plan B's threw me off, and detours shattered my hope for idealism. I wanted everyone to sit down for dinner together and on time. When people were late, and the food was cold, I was thoroughly disappointed. The moment was ruined. It didn't take much. When my dad brought this to my attention, I felt hurt. However, in retrospect, he was saving me from a life of heartache and letdowns. Now that I recognize this about myself, I've made mental adjustments that prepare me for those sand traps in life that are self-inflicted. I held life to idealistic measures, trying to control all the chess pieces around me with built-up beliefs that imperfect people could create a perfect day. Nowadays, I'm much more flexible and relaxed. I don't sweat the small stuff like I did in the past.

You can control life about as well as you can control the wind. Let it go: the balloons, the chains on the swing, the Norman Rockwell life. Remember, letting go of control doesn't mean that you don't care; it's just not an outcome you have the authority to steer. Only God does. "I do not consider myself to have taken hold of it," the Apostle Paul wrote. "But one thing I do, forgetting what is behind and reaching forward to what lies ahead" (Phil. 3:13). We may think that holding on makes us stronger, but sometimes it's in the letting go.

Four Questions to Letting Go

1. Why do you feel the need to micromanage your life or the lives of others?

2. What do you struggle with when trying to let go?

3. What one emotion would you feel if you gave up control?

4. If you didn't wait until life was perfect but started now, how would it feel?

My Prayer

Lord, when I am afraid, help me to put my trust in You, to quit steering a life that I have no authority to control. Help me to trust in You with my whole heart and truly let it go, knowing Your ways are higher than my ways. In Your Name, Amen.

CHAPTER 11
LIFE IS MAINTENANCE

I can do all things through Christ who strengthens me.

~Philippians 4:13~

I heard a scream in the upstairs bedroom. I ran like my life depended on it, touching only nine of seventeen steps before reaching the top. What I would find I didn't know, but I had to hurry. When I burst through the bedroom door, the sunset shining through the curtains illuminated the haze of orange dust that floated in the air. The screams of fear were actually screams of laughter. As my heart began to settle back into my chest, I found two enthusiastic toddlers and a baby in a white-spindled crib, jumping on a super-sized bag of Doritos crushed into powdered dust. They were laughing and squealing, covered in orange from head to toe. My surprise soon turned to anger. I had just given them baths, cleaned the room, and put them to bed. And now I had to start over. I never thought of myself as a girl who strived for perfection. But that's what I wanted: a life wrapped in a pretty red bow, like the last page of a fairytale children's book, before I closed my eyes for the evening. When would it ever end: the cooking, the cleaning, the laundry, and dishes? I have this running list of goals, checklists, and hope-tos, that include things like:

1. Sky diving before I'm fifty. (I pity the guy that tries to push me out.)

2. Getting back to my pre-baby weight before my youngest is ten—I mean, twelve.

3. Publishing a book to inspire moms before I'm walking with a cane.

4. Vacationing in Greece with all my favorite people. Yes!

The hope of a clean house at all times—well, that's not in the cards. I've walked a million miles in this house, picking up stuff, folding things, stepping on sharp objects, and looking for weird smells. I've washed countless dishes and made hundreds of lunches, and still, this house is full of piles. There's a clothes pile, a shoe pile, a toy pile, a book pile, and a miscellaneous pile. Like a game of whack-a-mole, as soon as one pile disappears, another pops up: containing a kid's sword, a space rocket sock that I never purchased, and two left flip flops. (For Christmas, I'd love a commercial-sized city trash bin placed in the backyard to use at my discretion. Ah, a girl can dream.) I notice, daily, the frustration of never getting all the laundry washed. There is always another dish to clean.

It never ends. This became a point of contention that kept me frustrated. Then one day, while getting the boys' haircuts, it dawned on me: life is maintenance. Nothing is ever done until the day we take our last breath. Mowing the lawn, trimming our nails, fueling the car, the honey-do list—it's all perpetual, never-ending. I wanted the slate wiped clean. I wanted the to-do list to be complete.

But it turns out, life is maintenance, and like death and taxes, laundry will be with you always. It's a mindset. Who runs to the front lawn every Thursday and screams, "When will this grass stop growing?" (Perhaps once you install turf.) If we can reconcile ourselves to the idea that life is maintenance and never ends, it won't be too hard of a pill to swallow. I love to have a clean house. I love a pristine kitchen and spotless windows. I love candles and vanilla smells. But if it stays this way for more than two days, it's probably because we're on vacation. One day, I spoke the words, "I will *not* have a clean house every day, and that's okay." But I didn't believe it. It wasn't "okay," which placed me in an odd predicament. What if we began to see life as maintenance, an ongoing-ness of sorts, rather than an endgame or goal to complete? Unless you're wearing disposable clothes, laundry is continuous. Quit killing yourself to finish a race that has no end. This is a lifetime marathon. Pace yourself and enjoy the journey.

When our family goes on road trips, my husband loves to see how fast he can drive from Point A to Point B. It's a game for him: "Hey babe, can we fuel up at exit 300 instead of 271? Do the kids *really* need to eat? Don't we have cheese in the car?" We skid into our destination mad, crazy, hot and hungry, as he celebrates beating his record by thirty-two seconds! All the hustling kept us from enjoying the journey, where all the goodness lives. It kept us from visiting the world's largest ball of twine. *What the what?* The joy is in the journey, not how fast we can run through it. So, stop thinking everything has to be perfect before it can start. Stop thinking you have to be the fastest, the greatest, the most put together. Stop thinking the kids can't leave home until they're all in matching outfits. Stop thinking you can't go to the grocery store until your makeup is perfect. There's always going to be something on the floor, in the sink. There's always going to be a kid with a dirty diaper, a teen with a bad attitude, a car that needs to be repaired, or a floor that needs to be vacuumed. Stop setting yourself up for failure by thinking otherwise. Life is not perfect; life is maintenance.

Do you remember the moment you gave perfectionism a starring role? The moment words like "regular" and "average" seemed so standard and subpar? Perfectionists seek to improve the welfare of those around them, seeking to make life better for the greater good. They set the bar high. Their method of communication is typically direct, with little patience for chit chat. The behavior of a perfectionist is driven by fear as they are desperately searching for validation, toeing the line in the form of a goodie two shoes or teacher's pet. It must be exhausting, never letting your guard down. If you are perfect, you are un-relatable to a large portion of the world, and as a boss or parent, you are seldom satisfied with others. Taking a risk is viewed as a weakness, and anything less than outstanding gets a failing grade. Let us find ways to exchange perfectionism with progress.

Prayer and counseling were key to changing my mindset. I carried emotional baggage from way back that told me *I'd never measure up*. Somewhere long ago, a story was written. Friends, family, classmates, my environment, an adult with their own issues of rejection and hurt. I clutched them all, like a squirrel collecting nuts for the winter. No matter the number of compliments and accolades, I couldn't receive them. My bucket carried only the negatives. My early years told me I was ugly, too loud, too much for some people, and not enough for others. People didn't like it when I established boundaries because it asserted too much power. Laughing and being funny brought me attention. So, I became a people pleaser, an entertainer, an achiever, hustling for my worth, climbing the corporate ladder higher and higher. *Can everyone see me? Look, I made it.* My resume was full of accomplishments and accolades. *Do you approve? Hey world, did I go high enough, far enough?* But guess what? I looked to the wrong people to fill up my cup, and those folks weren't giving affirmations today or any day. It actually made matters worse. It created a divide, a greater fracture. I spent my days filling a bucket full of holes.

I needed to be more, do more, prove more. I ran from my past. Striving to stay above the fray kept me isolated, exhausted, a hostage to the belief that I could be all and do it all. If I were fast enough, the house would always be clean. If I were something other than what I was, I would win the approval of those who couldn't give it. Once I realized I had nothing to prove, my guard came down.

I intentionally began to take risks and fail. And guess what? The earth didn't fall off its axis. I planned a small project that pushed me to the unknown. And guess what? The sky didn't fall. I apologized to myself and others, taking ownership of my mistakes. And guess what? People respected it. It taught me flexibility. It took grace and baby steps to see the progress. I'm no more special than the next guy. I'm a number like everyone else. I no longer had to prove my worth. I felt liberated. You can't outrun life. You're in a race with no end until you take your last breath. So, sit back, relax, and enjoy the ride.

When you mess up, seek forgiveness instead of justification. It's easy to spin plates with perfect precision for a few seconds. But for a lifetime, it's disastrous to you and those in your circle. Your poor adrenal glands can only take so much before they've sputtered out the last bit of cortisol, created for times of fight or flight. This will, in turn, deplete your progesterone, creating insomnia. This is a problem that counting sheep can't fix. It's like dangling a carrot you will never receive or seeking a treasure you will never find. It's a setup, a trap, the ultimate failure. A house can be clean, but not 24/7. If you have kids dropping toys, creating messes times two, three, and four, it becomes exponential. You'll find yourself in an angry mode all the time. Set down your overachieving self and pray. Pray for God to change your viewpoint. To let it go. To not be so, well, perfect—because you're *not actually* perfect.

Perfection is an ambush. You've raised the bar too high for mere mortals to win the game, which is good for you because you don't see yourself as a mere mortal. You come in to save the day and to show everyone how it's really done. You redo homework projects, rework their outfit, remake the meal, and rewash the dishes. When you stop expecting people to be perfect, you can accept them for who they are. Isn't that what you want for yourself?

Does everything have to be exactly right for you to proceed? It must be tough to hold on so tightly. Does maintaining a certain image hold you hostage from the goodness of the journey? Do you tell yourself, *If only I could create the perfect start, the perfect moment, then life can begin*? Perfection is without fault, flawless. I'm willing to bet you are neither of those things, no matter how much time you spend trying. Do you feel frustrated, less than, not quite measuring up? Perfectionism is a letdown; it ruins the moment. It says you're not enough and sends the same message to your family and peers.

What if I can't start something until the circumstances align correctly? News flash: they never will, and you'll never start. You'll miss out on the goodness of life. *What if people see that I'm not without flaws?* Well, guess what? They already know. *What if people catch me without makeup or see that my kids aren't perfect little creatures?* They'll think you're relatable.

You can do it. The power is within you, right here, right now. You are the only one holding you back. Get out of your way and flip the switch. Write down what needs to change and take baby steps to progress. Journal your hopes and dreams. This will be a game-changer for your family. Create a vision board for where you want to be in six months, one year, five years. What do you look like? How does your life feel? What you decide to do in this moment, at the fork in the road, will determine your legacy. Pray, seek counsel, and stay under God's refuge. He will give you wisdom. Living in the present provides rest for the weary, healing to the body, and peace for your soul. Be willing to do the work that allows you to sing in the rain, knowing that life is not perfect. It's just maintenance.

Four Steps to Creating a More Authentic Life

1. Name one thing that could help you let go of perfectionism.

2. List a small risk that's sure to fail and make a Plan B to create more flexibility.

3. Write down what happened when you apologized to your kids, how they reacted?

4. If the to-do list was not your boss, which humans would you spend more time with?

My Prayer

Lord, help me not to expect perfection in any area of my life (including the behavior of others), knowing that I'm just an imperfect creature like everyone else. Help me to let go of fear and control and to apologize when I'm wrong. Give me eyes to see that life is maintenance. It will always be filled with haircuts and laundry. Help me to not hurry through it all, trying to outrace life. Rather, help me know that I can do my best, and that is enough. In Your Name, Amen.

CHAPTER 12

THE POWER OF WRITING YOUR STORY

*Only one person is responsible for the quality of your life.
That is you.*

~Jack Canfield~

My Apple computer changed everything. Somewhere after Baby Number Three, my husband bought me a computer for our anniversary, fully loaded with video editing software. I scanned photos and added music, and before long, I had created my first digital scrapbook. It was so emotional and life-changing to hear the sounds of my kids' voices on the screen. Before long, I found myself creating videos for all my friends. We would meet for lunch and watch the video together. Tears were shed as their lives flashed before their eyes.

I wanted to create this moment for the entire universe. Who needs a shower on Day Three? I was changing the world, one saved memory at a time. Before long, friends were referring friends. What began as a passion quickly picked up steam.

On my son's first day of kindergarten, I wanted to follow him to all his classes, craft time, and recess. What a tough moment to let go of his little hand and pass it off to another. I was his entire world, and now I'd only be a piece of it. *Breathe girl, breathe.* By the time I walked to the car, I needed an intervention. I thought about him all day. Was he having fun? Did he get to swing? Had he made new friends? What story did they read during nap time?

So, I approached the principal and asked if I could create a "My First Day of Kindergarten" video as a school fundraiser. I would film all the Kindergartners as they moved from one class and activity to another. She agreed. This was my chance to see my son's day unfold without scouting him out with a set of binoculars from the school parking lot. (I'm totally kidding. Or am I?) We sent out homemade permission slips and interviewed every student with questions like, "What do you want to be when you grow up?" Y'all, I had no idea what I was doing. I borrowed a high-definition camera and hired a family member to help film. I had zero experience in videography or editing, only a passion for documenting family memories. Three days, two videographers, nine classes, 225 kids and twenty-one hours later, we began sifting through all the footage, questionnaires, and music, listening to little voices tell us how they wanted to be just like their mom or dad. It was sweetness personified.

Little did I know how many parents would find my cell number in the class directory, send emails, or show up at my front door with boxes of slides, videos, and pictures. I was just a mom wanting to share my passion for collecting kids' memories. In the beginning, I knew nothing about digitizing slides or 8 mm reels. It was overwhelming and unknown. As May approached, requests for graduation, reunion, and sports highlight reels hit their peak. My very first client was a dad from my son's elementary school whose father had passed away a day earlier. I didn't have an office, just a living room full of Legos. He stood at my front door, like a lost little boy, holding a box of tapes. With tears in his eyes, he sat in my living room, as two of my littles, still in diapers, ran around. He asked if I would create a celebration video for his dad's funeral. How could I say no? That's when I knew my "why." My passion for saving the world's memories had become a mission much greater than myself.

That fall, I rented a retail space, designed it to look like a beautiful living room setting, and opened up a business celebrating life's moments. My one-person video project became a full-fledged production company. Ignorance is bliss because I had no clue what I was getting myself into. But I had the courage and passion for walking towards my purpose. I had the determination to write my story. In the beginning, I had no idea how to transfer old reels to DVD. I had to educate myself, buy equipment, and slowly build up our service offerings. I had to learn how to brand our company, build a website, market services, hire an accountant, and develop a high school intern program. Before long, our staff began filming CEOs and posting their interviews to corporate sites, recording voiceovers, and creating annual sales videos for car companies and big-box stores. It all started when my husband saw something in me that I didn't—a gift for preserving moments. Launching a company brought exciting times, but it was not without difficulty or learning curves. Nothing comes without sacrifice.

There were risks, rewards, long nights, and frustrations in trying to build a business while raising a family. I learned that there's no such thing as work-life balance. It's a myth. I was on one end of the pendulum or the other. If I was helping a sick neighbor, dinner might take a backseat. If I was filing my taxes, laundry might have to wait. My husband had started a software company two years earlier that had its own growing pains, so this wasn't our first rodeo. It wasn't easy. We wore many hats, as the janitor, the accountant, the customer service representative, you name it, and we did it. We had to remind ourselves of our purpose—why we were doing all of this. We had to keep pushing forward, over and over, until we learned how to fly. There were nights we questioned ourselves and mentally dug each other out of the ditch.

We weren't just making videos; we were documenting memories. We got to commemorate stories of a parent whose child passed away from leukemia and that father broke down in my office, after never dealing with the pain. We got to document family histories, like siblings who discovered from boxes of old reels that they had a brother they had never met. Or grandchildren creating legacy videos for their ninety-five-year-old Jewish grandmother who had survived the Holocaust. There were so many moments of celebrations. I could hardly contain myself.

In the beginning, I didn't believe in me. I had no idea what I was doing or what I was capable of. I felt like a fraud. I had been a housewife six months earlier, and I had jumped off the corporate wagon long ago. But I had a husband, friends, and a community who believed in me. I stepped into my courage. I embraced my *why*, my reason, and learned how to create a company through a search engine and through taking risks that eventually paid off. I wrote my own story.

A few months before I sold the business, a mom from Indiana whose adult son was dying of cancer flew to Atlanta and filmed him interacting with his young children, playing, and reading books on the floor. Every day for weeks, she dropped off a video for me to transfer to DVD. We prayed together as she stared death in the face, dealing with her own debilitating health issues. Her daily visits eventually became a weekly ritual until one day she stopped. She called me on a rainy Wednesday and said her son's funeral was being held that morning. They showed a collection of those films from his last days at the memorial service. Months later, standing at a carwash with my four kids, as we watched the vehicles slowly move through the tunnel, a young woman with two littles, one on each hip, walked up and said, "You're the video girl, right?" I had no idea who she was. "You transferred my mother-in-law's videos for my husband before he passed away," she told me, "and for this, I will always be thankful."

Ladies, when you have a passion, walk towards it. When you have a dream burning in your soul, make room for it. It's not about you. It's about the world that you will (or won't) affect by moving forward (or not). Don't listen to the lies, the insecurities. Don't listen to the *I can't*s or excuses. Don't allow fear to run this ship. Fear is no bigger than a minnow in a fishin' hole. It has no power unless you give it. What is your superpower? Do you have an affinity for connecting people, designing software, writing stories, cooking, knitting, numbers, sales, editing, or architecture? All God wants is a willing vessel, and He will supply the rest. Jump, girl! Let go of the chains on that swing and jump. Remember, "I can do all things through Christ who gives me strength" (Philippians 4:13). You don't even have to go it alone.

God has your back. You're a team. It's time to walk in your purpose, sister.

First, write down your goals. Where do you want to be in one, three, or five years? Make them measurable. You'll need numbers, times, dates, and deadlines. (Read Michael Hyatt's book *Your Best Year Ever* to understand this concept better.) Make it as detailed as possible. Your dream may be much bigger than your current situation can handle. You have to make room for it. Secondly, research it. Map it out. Create a plan. And take the risk. Lastly, let go of other's expectations of what you should be. Don't allow others to define you.

We have this Goldendoodle, and her life's delight is to chase anything that flies: whether it's a butterfly, a bird, or a moth. If I demanded that she be a guard dog, she would fail on all levels, a disappointment to both parties. But allowing her to be what she was born for allows her to delight in what sparks her soul. There's freedom in walking in your true design.

What if God actually made you to be exactly the way you are with your personality, with your drive, the way you think, the way you sing, dance, design, and create? What if those negative comments aren't even about you, but about the person who spoke them, or who wrote them? Then it's their business, not yours. "Come to me," Jesus says, "all you who are weary and burdened, and I will give you rest. My yoke is easy and my burden is light" (Matthew 11:28 & 30). See, it's not your cross to bear. Jesus came to carry the burden for you. If you please others, you negate your uniqueness. God is the only one you need to please. Period. End of story. And when you focus on your lane and no one else's, the peace that passes all understanding will settle into your heart. Walk-in your greatness, sister. The world needs your perspective and personality. Be who you were made to be. You have always been enough. Go shine, girl.

But what if I walk away from my dream? What if I give up before it comes to fruition? Then you'll look back in five or ten years staring regret in the face. You will have stolen the goodness from those who needed your talent. Don't get in your own way. We tend to create habits that hold us hostage to the busyness of life. Instead of planning, leveraging, and taking action, we sit in our fear or in our comfort zone and hope for the best, believing it will all work out. Well, good luck with that. Great things don't just happen. Action is king. You can believe in something until the cows come home, but without action, there are no wheels to get you there. The destination, the career, the healthy body, the published book, the Etsy shop needs to be pointing in the right direction with momentum behind it. You can't steer a parked car.

What if Henry Ford had quit? What if he had opted out of designing the Model T because it was too difficult? Designing a car allowed Americans to visit national parks, created a transportation revolution, sparked capitalism, and influenced trade. The Wright Brothers had little money but a great drive to design the world's first flying machine. Their rivals had notoriety and hefty sponsorships, but on December 17, 1903, after building, crashing, failing, and trying over and over, these brothers successfully flew the world's first aircraft in Kitty Hawk, North Carolina, and no one was there to see it. There were no accolades or film crews, just hard work that paid off, day in and day out. What if they had decided it was too hard and taken an early retirement? Someone else would have invented the first plane, and the Wright Brothers would never be mentioned in the annals of history. Be the one: the change maker, the inventor, the creator, or the designer. There's enough room for all of us. Rise up and write your story.

You are more than a mom, a wife, a sister, or a daughter. That's a role you play, a position you hold. But it doesn't tell what burns within your soul. While you'll always be someone's someone, it's important to stay true to yourself and walk in your passion and purpose. You live only once. It takes courage and determination to walk into your greatness. What is the one thing that, if you don't walk towards it, will become a regret? While you're at a party on Friday night, someone else is running five miles in the dark to get those miles in after work, training for a marathon. While you're watching Netflix, someone else is watching tutorials on how to build a website. When you're waking up at 7 a.m., someone else has been writing their book since 5 a.m., before the day started. If you want results, you have to put in the time. You have to make room for the story you're creating. People will cheer you on, but they'll never be the jet fuel needed to take you to the next level. You have to be your own advocate, your own thrust to the finish line.

No one gets to tell you what your journey looks like or how your final story is written. You are the writer, the producer, and the director of all the parts. If you don't like how life is playing out, change it. If you want to start a business or get your Master's degree, do it. Start from where you are. There's no magical Monday. And someday is not a day on the calendar.

This may be your second or third act. You may think this is your final chapter. *You should have started earlier. Your time is running out. The train has left the station.* It's only true if you believe it. If you are alive and breathing, it's never too late to start now, where you are, at this moment.

Perhaps you've been raising kids for many years and want to jump back into the workforce. You've had this creative idea or product in your brain forever, and it's time to move forward or someone else will. You have a message in your heart that needs a pen placed to paper before your soul bursts. You have a need to paint, to express, to open an art studio. Do what it takes to make it happen. You might argue, *I've been out of the marketplace too long to make an impact; I'm no expert; I'm just a mom.* No, sister. They need your expertise, your years of problem-solving, mediating, and mad customer service skills. It's time to share with the world what you've learned. It's time to write your story.

It's easy to sit at home and wallow in your sorrows, thinking no one cares. It's easy to let others decide our fate. Remember the man cured of leprosy in the Bible? He followed Jesus through town on a mission to be healed. Determined to be seen, he weaved in and out of the crowd, inching his way closer. "Hey Leper, you don't belong here," villagers yelled. "Leave Jesus alone." Not today, Satan! He was persistent, 'til he finally grabbed Jesus' attention and begged for healing. Jesus placed His hands on the leper and because he believed, he was immediately healed. Can you imagine how much this changed his life? He no longer had to live on the outskirts of town, shunned socially. He was back in the land of the living. —back at his corporate job on Monday. ("Well, hello Fred, where have you been?") If he had listened to the crowd's opinion, he would still be living at Mt. Leprosy on the wrong side of the tracks. What changed? His belief. His tenacity. He didn't allow someone's no to become his answer. He didn't allow a little adversity to deny his dreams. He walked toward his purpose and found a better life.

It's easy to stay in your comfort zone and do nothing. Instead of saying, "I am the way I am, it is the way it is," be the change. This world is full of heartache and pain, but it's also full of opportunity and hopefulness. Want to change your life but don't know how? There are books, podcasts, sermons, videos, movies, TED Talks, and articles on any given topic to change your patterns and perspective. Perception is reality. It's the lens from which you'll view life. What you do with your story, how you create it is up to you. You have full editorial authority to compose your screenplay. When you look at the current state of your friendships, habits, work, and passion, what does it reflect? Look at your life. There are common threads that connect your gifts, talents, and dreams. Sewn together, they tell a greater story.

Is your life pieced together by tattered quilt squares that form an extraordinary tapestry, or is it a stack of misplaced pieces that will never fulfill their purpose? Both have similar squares, but one is repurposed for greatness. You might say, *I shouldn't reach for higher education because I'm not college material.* You may think, *Marriage equals pain* or *Finances equal lacking,* or *I was raised in the foster system; What could I offer?* It's time to change your lens and re-write your story. Pray, seek counsel. If you want to change, you have to create it. No one can do it for you. No one will care about your life, your hopes, and dreams like you will. No one. Not even those closest to you who were cheering you on at the beginning of the race. At some point, they walk away to tend to their own needs. You are the only one capable of unsnapping the lens on your viewfinder and replacing it with a clearer image. You are the only one that can turn tough times into positives lessons.

Are you hoping for change but walking the same path every day? The definition of *insanity* is doing the same thing over and over, expecting different results. Get out of the rut and build a new life. Change your circumstances.

Be intentional. Create a vision board and write down measurable goals to strategically map out where you are headed. You can't expect to go from here to there when you don't know where *there* is. Try placing *there* as your destination and see where it takes you. Quit wasting time justifying why you're still swirling in the same old circumstances. Stop listing your excuses. No one wants to hear them. You're burning precious daylight, sister. There is not a single place on earth that you can't get to from where you are if you map out the destination. It may take a business class, working a second job, or getting some experience under your belt. But the starting line is where you are standing.

Tough times in the valley make for sweeter victories on the mountain top. Every time you fall down and get back up, you're reminded of what you're made of. "Let us not become weary in doing good," we read in Galatians 6:9, "for at the proper time, we will reap a harvest of blessing if we do not give up." A forward fall is winning. Be thankful for the new life you're walking towards, because you don't want to ever go back from where you came. People will tell stories of surviving abuse, divorce, a cross-country move, a job change, losing friends, the death of a child or spouse, and they come out on the other side as motivational speakers, nutritionists, physical therapists, and influencers.

Don't use your past to justify your inaction. Instead, use your past to produce the very thing you want to give back to the universe. Allow your pain to become your platform. Don't use your situation as a crutch. Instead, thank it for making you the person you've become. The life you seek will not occur by happenstance, but if you're walking towards it with vision and purpose, doing the hard things, your vibe will attract your tribe. No matter your age, your race, or your geography, no matter when or how you start, the world needs your version of the story, your talent, your gift. Stay the course, keep knocking, keep pressing. Never give up. "For I know the plans that I have for you, declares the Lord, plans to prosper you and not to harm you. Plans to give you a future and a hope" (Jeremiah 29:11). You are both a mess and a masterpiece—and you have always been enough. It's time to step into your greatness, girl, and write your story. Here's to living your best life.

Four Ways to Change Your Perspective

1. In an effort to create good habits, what two routines could you focus on this week?

2. Write five items in your journal that you are grateful for; do this daily.

3. List four people who make you want to be a better person than you were yesterday.

4. If you are the average of the five people you hang around, would you change any of those friends?

My Prayer

Lord, in Isaiah 55:11 it says, "The Word goes out from my mouth and will not return empty but will accomplish what I desire and achieve the purpose for which it is sent." Help me to rely on your scripture and be thankful for how the past has influenced who I am today. Help me not to complain or blame, but to find solutions and have a grateful heart—so that when this life I lead is over, I will not have a single regret. I will have lived life to the fullest, with my arms open wide. In Your Name, Amen.

LIKE THIS BOOK?

Consider:

- ~ Sharing it with a friend/social media or on a blog

- ~ Utilizing the questions as a study group

- ~ Writing a review

- ~ Recommending to your church, business, rotary group, women's conference or book club

Share your stories and your wins with us at: #LivingYourBestLifeBook

Connect with Stephanie:
Instagram @stephaniepletka
FB Stephaniepletka,writer
Website: StephaniePletka.com

Want Stephanie to Speak at Your Event? Stephanie@ StephaniePletka.com

Subscribe to stephaniepletka.com/contact to receive encouraging emails, tips and bonus material.

Discussion Questions:

Download the PDF at stephaniepletka.com/livingyourbestlife for small group use.

Available where all books are sold.

ACKNOWLEDGMENTS

To John, the love of my love, the one I met on a bus all those years ago. Thanks for helping me dream big and go for all those crazy ideas in my head. Life with you is an incredible adventure! To my tribe, the Hoot and Holler Club, I want to thank: Karen, Shelly, Kim, Lori, Zelda, Jennifer, Misty, Charlene, Jana, Amy, Susan and Sherry for bringing joy, laughter and meaning to my life. Community and connection are the reason for it all. I'd like to thank Susan Miller for helping me pick up the pieces when this Southern girl moved from Georgia to the Arizona desert. You helped me bloom where I was planted. Thanks for walking towards your passion and establishing JustMoved.com ministries to help women successfully navigate change. Thanks to Kary Oberbrunner, my publisher at Author Academy Elite, to Nanette, Brenda, Abigail, and Nicci for answering all my questions and walking along side me on this journey. Thank you to my editors, Susan Pohlman, Emily Wooten, Teresa Baumbach and Laura Zeitner for making me look like a professional and sticking with me, when I had no clue what I was doing. I'd like to thank my parents who taught me tenacity, to take risks, to pick myself up by the boot straps and try again. And to my dad who taught me the art of good story telling. To Wadie, my surrogate Alabama grandma who took this eleven year old girl under her wing and gave me confidence to fly. To Daryl who encouraged me through the teen years, that God had a plan for my life, giving me hope for the future. I'd like to give a shout out to my Granny who embraced my wild spirit, a safe place that allowed me to just be me. And finally, I'd like to thank God, who's captured every tear, listened to every prayer and with arms wide open and hands full of grace, redemption and forgiveness, reminded me - that who I am is who I was always meant to be.

NOTES

1. Tim Ferriss, *Tools of the Titans* (New York: Publisher Houghton Mifflin Harcourt 2016).

2. Dr. Juliana Breines, *The Perils of Comparing Ourselves to Others* (Psychology Today, https://www.psychologytoday.com/us/blog/in-love-and-war/201607/the-perils-comparing-ourselves-others)

3. Dr. Henry Cloud, *Necessary Endings* (Harper Collins, January 2011).

4. Lysa TerKeurst, *The Best Yes* (Thomas Nelson, August 2014).

5. Dr. Henry Cloud, *Boundaries* (Zondervan, February 2018).

6. Tyler Perry, *Madea Character The Tree Speech Let "Em Go* (YouTube video. http://Vimeo.com/86149821)

7. Bob Goff, *Love Does* (goodreads.com/author/quotes/5758647.bob_goff)

8. Steve Harvey, *Jump* (Amistad, September 2017).

9. Thomas Edison Quote, (brainyquote.com/quotes/thomas_a_edison_132683).

10. Teddy Roosevelt, *Man in the Arena Speech* (www.worldatlas.com/articles/man-in-the-arena.html)

11. Kyle Idleman, *Grace is Greater* (Baker Books February 2017).

12. Shauna Niequist, *Present Over Perfect* (Zondervan, August 2016).

13. Rick Warren, *Let Go and Know God is in Control* (https://pastorrick.com/let-go-and-know-god-is-in-control/).

14. Susan Miller, *After the Boxes are Unpacked* (April 1, 2016)

15. Coco Chanel (www.goodreads.com/quotes/7121021-beauty-begins-the-moment-you-decide-to-be-yourself)

16. Gary Smalley, *The Heart of Remarriage* (Revel, November 2015)

17. Gary Chapman, *The 5 Love Languages* (Northfield Publishing January 2015)

18. Laird Hamilton, www.goodreads.com/quotes/7834156-make-sure-your-worst-enemy-doesn-t-live-between-your-own).

19. Grace Hansen, (https://www.mrgreatmotiva-tion.com/2018/05/dont-be-afraid-your-life-wil l-end-be.html).

20. Ferriss Bueller, *Ferriss Bueller's Day Off Movie* (Paramount Pictures June 1986).

21. Interview with moms Upworthy.com (July 7, 2014, https://www.upworthy. com/these-kids-finally-say-what-the y-really-think-about-mom-and-he r-reaction-priceless-9)

22. Bernard Baruch (https://www.goodreads. com/quotes/865-be-who-you-are-an d-say-what-you-feel-because).

23. Jack Canfield, (https://www.jackcanfield.com/ blog/taking-100-responsibility-for-your-life/).

CPSIA information can be obtained
at www.ICGtesting.com
Printed in the USA
FFHW021646171219
57055124-62645FF